Monks and Muslims

MONASTIC INTERRELIGIOUS DIALOGUE SERIES

Monks and Muslims

Monastic and Shiʿa Spirituality in Dialogue

Edited by
Mohammad Ali Shomali
and
William Skudlarek

LITURGICAL PRESS
Collegeville, Minnesota

www.litpress.org

Cover design by David Manahan, OSB.

Unless otherwise noted, translations from non-English sources are provided by the respective authors in this book.

1 2 3 4 5 6 7 8 9

Library of Congress Cataloging-in-Publication Data

Monks and Muslims : monastic and Shiʿa spirituality in dialogue / edited by Mohammad Ali Shomali and William Skudlarek.
p. cm. — (Monastic interreligious dialogue series)
Includes bibliographical references.
ISBN 978-0-8146-3442-4 — ISBN 978-0-8146-3443-1 (ebook)
1. Islam—Relations—Christianity. 2. Christianity and other religions—Islam. 3. Shiʿah—Doctrines. 4. Theology, Doctrinal. 5. Dialogue—Religious aspects—Islam. 6. Dialogue—Religious aspects—Christianity. I. Shomali, Mohammad A., 1965– II. Skudlarek, William.

BP172.M645 2012
261.2'7—dc23

2012011863

Contents

Introduction vii

Chapter 1: Revelation

A Monastic Perspective on Divine Revelation 1
Benoît Standaert, OSB

A Shi^cite Perspective on Divine Revelation 10
Mohammad Ali Shomali

Chapter 2: Lectio Divina

A Monastic Perspective on *Lectio Divina* 27
Guido Dotti

A Shiʿite Perspective on *Lectio Divina* 35
Farrokh Sekaleshfar

Chapter 3: Prayer

A Monastic Perspective on Prayer 47
Lucy Brydon, OSB

A Shiʿite Perspective on Prayer 58
Fatemeh Nazari

A Shiʿite Perspective on Ritual Prayer 75
Mohammad Taghi Ansaripour

Chapter 4: Public Prayer

A Monastic Perspective on Public Prayer 87
Notker Wolf, OSB

A Shiʿite Perspective on Public Prayer 96
Mahnaz Heydarpoor

Chapter 5: Witness within the Community

A Monastic Perspective on Living in Community 107
Julian Pieters, OCSO

A Shiʿite Perspective on the Life of the Muslim *Ummah* 117
Abbas Jaffer

Chapter 6: Witness in the World

A Monastic Perspective on Giving Witness in a Secular World 124
Finbarr Dowling, OSB

A Shiʿite Perspective on Giving Witness in a Secular World 133
Mohsen Javadi

Chapter 7: Dialogue

Monastic-Muslim Dialogue: The Challenge and the Promise 143
Timothy Wright, OSB

Dialogue: A Bridge between the Oneness of God and the Unity of Humanity 150
Mohammad Ali Shomali

Selected Bibliographies 157

List of Contributors 161

Introduction

The first formal meeting for dialogue between Catholic monks and nuns and Iranian Shiʿa Muslims took place in England in 2003. Chapter 7 of this book describes how a chance encounter in 2001 was the beginning of a decade of ever-deepening knowledge, friendship, and trust between followers of these two ancient and illustrious spiritual traditions that until then had been virtually unknown to one another.

That first formal meeting of Benedictine monks and nuns with Iranian Shiʿa Muslims was devoted to the topic of spirituality and theology and was referred to by the Catholic periodical *The Tablet* as "the first major British encounter of Catholic theologians with Iranian Shiʿa thinkers and theologians."[1] Two more conferences followed: the second on faith and reason and the third on ethics.[2] While these meetings were a Benedictine-Muslim initiative and hosted in the Benedictine abbeys of Ampleforth and Worth, they were conducted in collaboration with Heythrop College of the University of London and included participants from beyond the Benedictine world.

[1] *The Tablet*, 19 July 2003, 13.

[2] The proceedings of all three conferences were recently reissued by Melisende Publishing in London: *Catholics and Shiʿa in Dialogue: Studies in Theology and Spirituality* (2004); *A Catholic-Shiʿa Engagement: Faith and Reason in Theory and Practice* (2006); *A Catholic-Shiʿa Dialogue: Ethics in Today's Society* (2008).

In addition to the three formal meetings that took place in England, monks and theologians from England visited Iran in 2002, 2004, and 2006, made presentations in various institutes in Qum, engaged in informal but penetrating dialogue with faculty and students, and were warmly received wherever they went.

The focus of this most recent dialogue has now been directed toward the spiritual practices and religious experience of Christian monasticism and Shiʿa Islam. The meeting was held in September 2011 at the Primatial Abbey of Sant'Anselmo in Rome, the center of the Benedictine world, and was sponsored by Monastic Interreligious Dialogue, an international organization that promotes and supports dialogue, especially dialogue at the level of religious experience and practice, between Christian monastic men and women and followers of other religions. The Christian participants were monastic and came from nine different countries in Africa, Europe, and North America. The Muslim participants were Iranian and British Shiʿa, most of whom live in Iran, all of whom are professors, postgraduate students, and graduates of universities and seminaries in Qum.

Those who read monastic periodicals like *The American Benedictine Review*, *Erbe und Auftrag*, or *Studia Monastica* will find little on the relationship between Muslim and monastic spirituality. The silence of the monastic world vis-à-vis Islam has become less deafening in recent years, thanks to the witness of Christian de Chergé and the Cistercian community of Tibhirine, Algeria. The uniqueness of Christian de Chergé was that he had a degree from the Pontifical Institute for Arabic and Islamic Studies (PISAI) in Rome, which enabled him to weave into his monastic conferences appropriate references from the Qurʾan. His death, along with six of his brethren, brought an untimely end to the community at Tibhirine and to his initiatives, but it did awaken recognition that Christian monks—and Christians in general—need to become aware and appreciative of the rich spiritual resources of Islam.

A remark of Frithjof Schuon will help to understand why it is important for Christian monks and Muslims to become friends who are willing to speak of their own religious practice and experience and who are eager to listen to and learn from one another. In his article "The Universality of Monasticism and Its Relevance in the Modern World" he first poses the question "Why is monasticism excluded from a religion which nevertheless possesses mysticism, ascetic discipline, and a cult of saints?" He offers this answer:

> One of the *raisons d'être* of Islam is precisely the possibility of a "monastery-society," if the expression is allowable: that is to say that Islam aims to carry the contemplative life into the very framework of society as a whole; it succeeds in realizing within that framework conditions of structure and of behavior that permit of contemplative isolation in the very midst of the activities of the world. . . . The famous "no monasticism in Islam" (*lâ rahbâniyah fî-islâm*) really means, not that contemplatives must not withdraw from the world, but on the contrary that the world must not be withdrawn from contemplatives; the intrinsic ideal of monasticism or of eremitism, namely asceticism and the mystical life, is in no way affected.[3]

The 2011 conference was a response to Schuon's implicit invitation to monastics and Muslims to learn from and encourage one another, and the papers given there and presented here certainly lay a foundation. But there is still much work to be done. The ongoing challenge is that monastic and Muslim communities become ever more deeply involved in this uncharted area, to which they both bring centuries of wisdom and expertise.

Mohammad Ali Shomali
Timothy Wright, OSB
William Skudlarek OSB

[3] In Rob Baker and Gray Henry, *Merton and Sufism* (Louisville, KY: Fons Vitae, 2005), appendix C, p. 322.

Chapter 1

Revelation

A Monastic Perspective on Divine Revelation

Benoît Standaert, OSB

A monk in the tradition of Saint Benedict, the founder of our monastic family, is supposed to read from the Bible, both the Old Testament and the New, for an hour or more every day.

Lectio Divina

This practice is called *lectio divina*, "divine reading." Translated literally, the term means "reading God," the word "divine" standing here for the object of our reading. The expression *lectio divina* is usually not translated. A translation did exist in Greek—θεία ἀναγνώρισις (*theia anagnôrisis*)—at the time of the church fathers (from the fourth to the fifth centuries), but in modern languages there is no apt equivalent, and so we prefer to keep to the Latin expression.

What is shocking about this formula is that we should "read *God*"! The root meaning of *lectio/leg(g)ere—lire* in French, *lesen* in German, *lezen* in Dutch—is "binding" or "collecting," like λόγος (*logos*) and λέγειν (*legein*) in Greek. But how can we collect or *bind* God? The reality, on the level of experience, is that we *are read* by God, brought together and recollected *by God* in our act of reading.

So, within the traditional expression for the prayerful reading of Scripture we may already find an opening to the deep mystery of our effective relationship to the living God.

Revelation

How do we experience the *revelation* of God in and through this practice? An old saying makes it clear: "When you read, he speaks to you; when you pray, you speak to him." We find this saying in the writings of Saint Cyprian, Saint Jerome, and Saint Augustine, three major Latin church fathers who lived between 300 and 430.

Lectio and *oratio*—reading and prayer—are joined together in this exercise like the act of breathing. Just as there is no inhalation without exhalation, so there is no prayer without reading and no reading without praying.

The purpose of our reading is not just to comprehend (to "grasp") the text by intelligence, analysis, comparison, synthesis. We read to listen to Someone and to enter into a kind of conversation with him. From the practice of reading we receive light, meaning, impulse, direction, sense. Our first attitude is one of receptivity rather than grasping.

The Vigan Method

Today there is a method of *lectio divina* for small groups (six people maximum) that originated in the Philippines and has spread throughout the world. We call it the "Vigan Method,"

Vigan being the city from which the method was circulated by the catechetical center of John Paul I. Sister Henrietta Sebastian, a Benedictine nun who later became abbess of her community, and Father Ludger Feldkämper, a German priest of the Divine Word Missionary Society, proposed the method at the end of the 1970s. I have found it very helpful and have used it with groups of lay people for more than twenty years.

The method comprises three steps—Text, Word, Response—and each step has three moments: Reading, Silence, Sharing. For each step, however, there is a different question to be answered:

1. *Text:* What are the expressions that strike me?
    a. Read the text aloud.
    b. Reflect in silence.
    c. Respond with a simple statement without comment.
2. *Word:* What is the Lord saying to me through this text, here and now?
    a. Read the text aloud.
    b. Reflect in silence.
    c. Respond.
3. *Response:* What is my response to what the Lord says to me?
    a. Read the text aloud.
    b. Reflect in silence.
    c. Respond in the form of a prayer that eventually leads to a personal engagement.

The second step is the difficult one: How do we allow the text to become the Word of God? It is a question not of grasping with the mind but of pure listening with the heart. To avoid personal considerations *about* the text, we always introduce the sharing of that second step with, "The Lord says to me: 'Benoît, [we each say our own name] . . .' "

This method of reading the Scriptures, proposed for groups of five or six people, can also be used when one is reading the Bible alone or even when one is preparing a homily.

The basic theological insight behind the Vigan Method is that of the church fathers and of the Bible itself: our God is speaking. Continuously. But do we hear him? Is there a connection? Or is our line always busy, making it impossible for him to get through? So we try to be more receptive to God's speaking to us when we come together to hear his Word or when we read in silence the text of the Divine Word, as we call it.

As you may have noticed, the inner rhythm of the Vigan Method parallels the sequence of our three days together: Word, Prayer, and Action by Witness.

Saint Benedict, the founder of our monastic tradition, used the image of light to describe his approach to God's Word: reading and listening is much like looking attentively to the divine light. In the Prologue to his Rule he writes, "*attentis oculis ad deificum lumen*" ("our eyes open to the light that comes from God," or "to the light that makes us like God"). In fact, the very first word of God in Holy Scripture, spoken on the first day of creation, is "Let there be light!" (יהי אור, *Yehi ʿor*; Gen 1:3). But is it not true that every one of God's words is *lumen de lumine* ("light out of Light")?

The Revelatory Dimension throughout Our Entire Life

The practice of *lectio divina* is essentially revelatory, and this revelation affects our whole being and shapes the attitude we bring to every possible situation.

Let it be clear, when we as monks approach the Gospel, the Psalms, the Torah of Moses, or the Prophets, we do not become involved in discussions about the degree to which these words, these sayings and stories, are precisely inspired by the Holy Spirit. There are academies where scholars can formally debate those questions. But a monk, generally speaking, is not at all concerned with them.

One of the reasons for the monk's lack of interest in these historical/critical questions is that the church recommends that all the books of the Bible be read as the Word of God. Believers of the past have experienced the value of this literature, and for this reason certain writings of the first followers of Christ were selected as authoritative for Christian believers. Over the centuries all twenty-seven books of the New Testament and the many books of the First Testament in Hebrew and in Greek were copied and circulated. As monks, we basically trust that ancient decision.

However, monks do not want to limit the revelatory dimension of human experience to sacred and authoritative texts. For them God speaks everywhere and all the time. Their human consciousness is open to the divine consciousness and attentive to the possibility of revelation in any event of life. Here we may perceive an essential element of spiritual consciousness: once we realize plainly the light of our own consciousness, we perceive a direct door to the divine consciousness as a light that supports our interiority and self-consciousness but that has in itself no beginning and no end. The act of reading is—at least for some monks—rooted in this perception of their participation in the divine Act of Being.

Giving a privileged position to some texts as revelatory in the name of God does not mean that we are suspicious about other literature or even about other ways of approaching reality with an open mind. In a certain way, our experience is just the opposite. The sacred text itself gives us keys and tools to deal with all reality as an open book in which the face of God is revealed. In the Rule of Saint Benedict we find that the guest, the sick person, the poor at the door, the elder, and the child are all possible *revelations* of Christ. There is divine revelation in daily life, as Jesus makes clear when he says, "I was sick and you took care of me. . . . Truly I tell you, just as you did it to one of the least of these who are members of my family, you did it to me" (Matt 25:36, 40).

We can also recall the occasion when Jesus was sitting at the entrance of the temple and saw a poor widow making an offering of just two small coins of no value at all. "Then he called his disciples and said to them, 'Truly I tell you, this poor widow has put in more than all those who are contributing to the treasury. For all of them have contributed out of their abundance; but she out of her poverty has put in everything she had, all she had to live on' " (Mark 12:43-44).

The strength of this remark is that the widow was not a follower of Jesus. She remained in her own tradition, faithful to the rites going on in the temple, which Jesus had earlier rejected. Can we look on other believers with the eyes of Jesus? For example, when we see a Hindu entering a shrine with some fruit and flowers to offer, can we, like Jesus, appreciate the full gift of life that is expressed in that gesture of offering? So we see how Scripture teaches us to receive revelation even from outside our own tradition.

Revelation in Reciprocity

Moreover, in the Rule of Saint Benedict the sick person is regarded as Christ, but so is the visitor. Around the sickbed there is an opportunity for Christ to meet Christ in pure reciprocity, the highest and most beautiful form of revelation in life. If we consider the entire model of life in the Rule, we could say that monks are in fact trained to this way of perceiving divine reciprocity by seeing Christ in the sick, the guest, the child, and the abbot. We obey the abbot, in whom we hear Christ. But Christ is also present in the response of the obedient monk, who is to have in his heart the words of Christ who said, "I have come down from heaven, not to do my own will, but the will of him who sent me" (John 6:38).

For monks, the practice of praying the psalms offers a privileged way of receiving divine revelation. The psalms are the Word of God in the words of men. We pray them "in Christ" and we pray them "to Christ." Saint Augustine has made clear that this original reciprocity is rooted in our faith that we are the Body of Christ. Christ assumes all the suffering of humanity, suffering that is so poignantly expressed in the words of the psalms, but Christ, as head of the body, is also the one to whom we may confidently address all our desires and supplications.

During these past few days I stayed in a Benedictine community here in Rome where a brother had just died. When, after his death, we prayed the psalms, we also prayed them in his name: the "I" of the psalm became, in Christ, the "I" of that brother who expects to be received into the eternal dwelling place that God has prepared for him.

We could even refer here to the liturgical practice of the celebration of the Eucharist. When the community gathers together to celebrate the Eucharist and the Word of God is publicly proclaimed and then related to the life the community through the homily (preaching), we may hear a revelatory message for this very moment. In addition, our gestures and our repetition of what Jesus said and did when he took the bread and broke it on the night before he died—"While they were eating, Jesus took a loaf of bread, and after blessing it he broke it, gave it to the disciples, and said, 'Take, eat; this is my body' " (Matt 26:26)—allow us to perceive again a strange and unique reciprocity: he in us and we in him act out and fulfill the form as well as the content of what was said then and is now repeated in the present celebration.

We meet the revelatory dimension of life everywhere—in the humblest tasks of serving at the table, as well as in the most solemn gestures of a liturgical celebration. In a certain way, it makes no difference. Saint Benedict counsels the cellarer (bursar or steward) of the monastery to "regard all utensils and goods of the monastery as sacred vessels of the altar" (RB 31.10). The holy books of the Bible, it is true, do offer us a privileged access to divine revelation, but the God who is revealed there is a God who calls us to open our eyes to the divine light, wherever and whenever it shines.

Hospitality or Humble Openness to Any Otherness

This understanding of revelation provides a theological opening for us as monks to appreciate other holy books and other religious traditions. We may make mistakes, but we learn from them and remain open. Our openness is rooted in the Gospel and in texts of our monastic tradition. That may be not enough for some academic theologians, but we would like to invite them to join us on the level of life shared with the poor, the stranger, the *anawim*, the humble, the *fakirs* of all other religious traditions. A strong spiritual intuition makes us sure about one thing: the humble monk, the poor rabbi, the unassuming Buddhist *bhikkhuni*, the transparent Hindu *sannyasi*, and the authentic Muslim *fakir* will never fight. They can only enlarge peace on earth.

We may need to remind scholars that, without any pretention, the humble are always in advance of most schools or academies. They are prophets. Not everybody may like to hear this kind of "prophecy." But as Jean Vanier, the founder of communities for and with handicapped people (L'Arche), has often insisted, the humblest and poorest person in a community is the most prophetic. Can we be open to one another and accept that the other is also, in his or her own person and as a bearer of a religious tradition, an authentic *revelation* of the Invisible?

This is the understanding to which the practice of *lectio divina* has brought us. I think here of something Christian de Chergé, the prior of Tibhirine (Algeria), wrote about one of his Muslim friends:

> Since the day he asked me, quite unexpectedly, to teach him how to pray, M. has gotten into the habit of coming to see me. Thus we have built a longstanding spiritual exchange. . . . One day he discovered that he could get my attention by saying, "It's been a long time since we have dug our wells!" We use this expression when we feel the need for a deeper level of conversation. Once, in a joking way, I asked him, "And what will we find at the bottom of our well? Muslim water or Christian water?" He looked at me with an expression that was both pained and amused: "You are still asking that question? Do you still not understand that what you find at the bottom of this well is the water of God?"[1]

[1] *Sept vies pour Dieu et l'Algérie*, Textes recueillis et présentés par Bruno Chenu (Paris: Bayard/Centurion, 1996), p. 46.

In both of our traditions we have the example of Abraham to show us how to receive, in a spirit of true hospitality, the otherness of the other as we would receive the Lord himself. Abraham's guests at the oak of Mamre were just passers-by, but he received them as the Lord and was blessed by a divine promise that is still a blessing for all the descendants of the one who was born out of that hospitality, including you and us, Muslims and Christians.[2]

Pilgrims Walking under One Shoulder

The prophet Zephaniah was convinced that only a remnant of poor, humble people will be left on God's mountain. They will come from all nations and will join together as pilgrims, no one dominating anyone else. They will "walk under one shoulder," or "shoulder to shoulder"[3] (Zeph 3:9, 12). May this prophetic vision that is about twenty-seven centuries old inspire us for today and tomorrow![4]

Peace. Salam. Shalom. Shanti. Pax. Vrede.

[2] The relationship of monastic hospitality to interreligious dialogue has been developed by Pierre-François de Béthune in his book *Interreligious Hospitality: The Fulfillment of Dialogue* (Collegeville, MN: Liturgical Press, 2010).

[3] This passage is cited in *Nostra Aetate* (4). "Shoulder to shoulder" is a literal translation of the phrase in Zephaniah 3:9 that is translated "and serve him with one accord" in the NRSV.

[4] I have developed these ideas further in *Sharing Sacred Space: Interreligious Dialogue as Spiritual Encounter* (Collegeville, MN: Liturgical Press, 2009), pp. 54–56, and in "Welcoming and Being Welcomed into Each Other's Space," in *The Attentive Voice: Reflections on the Meaning and Practice of Interreligious Dialogue*, ed. William Skudlarek (New York: Lantern Books, 2011), pp. 112–13.

A Shiᶜite Perspective on Divine Revelation

Mohammad Ali Shomali

All adherents of the Abrahamic faiths believe that God has communicated with certain people, known as the prophets, so that they may guide humankind toward happiness.[1] In what follows, I will refer briefly to the main elements of the Muslim understanding of this communication in general and of the divine communication to Prophet Muhammad as embodied in the Qurᵓan in particular.

Definition of *Wahy*

For a more precise understanding of the Islamic perspective on divine revelation or word of God, it is necessary to become acquainted with the term *wahy*. In Arabic this term literally means giving a message quickly and secretly, whether by gesture, in a written form, or by inspiration.[2] The term has been

[1] An early edition of this paper was initially presented to an interfaith conference in Krakow, Poland, in November 2004 on "Sacred Books and the Word of God." An expanded version of that presentation was published in *Islamochristiana* in 2007 (no. 33, pp. 121–136), entitled "Divine Revelation: A Shīᶜa Perspective on Divine Guidance and Human Understanding." This is an updated and selected version of that paper.

[2] E.g., see *Mufradaat Alfaz al-Qurᵓan*, p. 858; *Al-Sihaah*, vol. 6, p. 2519; *Al-Qaamus al-Muhit*, vol. 4, p. 399.

used in this sense both before the advent of Islam (e.g., in pre-Islamic poetry) and after it. There is also a technical sense in which the term *wahy* is used to denote "communication of God to the prophets."

In the Qur'an, the term *wahy* or one of its cognates occurs seventy-eight times and is used in a broad sense. Except for five, all of these cases pertain to God as giver of the message.[3] Therefore, the first thing that comes to mind is that the concept is used primarily for divine revelation in the Qur'an, though there is also a more general sense of conveying any message. With regard to the verses in which the term or one of its cognates is used to refer to the divine act of giving messages, the recipients of this communication are

1. Prophet Muhammad: he is the paradigmatic recipient of *wahy* as mentioned in the Qur'an, and nearly half the cases in which the term *wahy* or its cognates are used in the Qur'an relate to him;
2. the Prophets, of whom Moses is most frequently mentioned;
3. the disciples of Jesus or the mother of Moses;
4. angels;
5. the bee; and
6. the heavens.

As we see, *wahy* is not restricted to the prophets. Rather, it is used in a more general sense to refer to different sorts of guidance given by God to His creatures, and since divine guidance is all-inclusive, His *wahy* reaches out to all forms of creation. The

[3] One of those exceptions is related to Zechariah. When he received the good news of having a child, he asked God for a sign. The sign was not being able to talk for three nights. So when he went out of the temple, instead of talking to the people, he *awha*—i.e., he *signaled* to the people to glorify God morning and evening (19:11).

Qur'an teaches that God, the Wise, has provided His creatures with guidance so that they may achieve their proportionate perfection. The first form of divine guidance is an inner and instinctive instruction, which is innate in all beings. It is from Him that each created thing derived its form and nature, including the free will and power that was given to human beings. God has granted to everything all the means and opportunities for development. The Qur'an says:

> He said, "Who is your Lord, Moses?" He said, "Our Lord is He who gave everything its creation and then guided it." (20:49-50)

> Celebrate the Name of your Lord, the Most Exalted, who created and proportioned, who determined and guided. (87:1-3)

The second form of divine guidance is through the prophets and divine books that teach men and women why they were created and how they can realize their true potential. The prophets inform people of what is outside the realms of their knowledge and experience, explain to them the consequences of their actions, confirm and support what they can understand through reason, and serve as a role model for them to follow. Thus, human beings enjoy two sorts of guidance: the general guidance (*al-hidāyat al-ʿāmmah*), which is shared by all creatures, and the special guidance (*al-hidāyat al-khāssah*), which is exclusive to those beings that have reason and free will. This form of divine communication to human beings through the prophets is called *wahy* by Muslim theologians.

The occurrences of divine *wahy* in the Qur'an can also be classified according to the nature of the messages into the following categories.

Natural instinct. We always admire the wonderful achievements of small insects, such as bees, ants, spiders, and so forth.[4]

[4] The Qur'an says: "And thy Lord taught the Bee to build its cells in hills on trees and in [human] habitations; Then to eat of all the produce [of the earth] and find with skill the spacious paths of its Lord: there issues from within their bodies a drink of varying colors wherein is healing for men:

The same is true about the laws of nature, such as gravity or the movement of atoms, planets, and so on. This is all due to a general guidance provided by God.

Inspiration. Sometimes God suggests certain ideas or courses of action to some people who are not necessarily prophets.[5] For example, we read in the Qur᾽an that in order to protect Moses, God inspired (*awhaynā*) his mother to put the baby in the river.[6] This inspiration was not conveyed through an angel, and the mother of Moses was not a prophet. Therefore, there is also a kind of general inspiration for all people. For example, the Qur᾽an tells us that God has inspired humans to be able to discern between virtues and vices (91:8).

Prophetic revelation. This is exclusive to the prophets and is referred to in the Qur᾽an more than seventy times.[7] For example:

> Thus have We revealed to you an Arabic Qur᾽an that you may warn [the people of] the Mother of the Towns and those around it, and warn [them] of the Day of Gathering, in which there is no doubt, [whereupon] a part [of mankind] will be in paradise and a part will be in the Blaze. (42:7)

---

verily in this is a Sign for those who give thought" (16:68-69). *Wahy* here consists in divine instructions about where to live, what to eat, and what sort of behavior to have.

[5] The Qur᾽an tells us that Satan and his followers also engage in counter-inspiration. E.g., verse 6:121 reads as follows: "But the evil ones inspire their friends to contend with you; if you were to obey them you would indeed be pagans."

[6] E.g., the Qur᾽an says, "So we sent this inspiration to the mother of Musa: 'Suckle the child, but when you have fears about him, cast him into the river, but fear not, nor grieve; for We shall restore him to you, and We shall make him one of the messengers' " (28:7; see 20:37-40).

[7] In addition to using the term *wahy* to refer to prophetic revelation, the Qur᾽an frequently (more than two hundred times) uses cognates with the root (*nuzul*) meaning: "descending." In its transitive form, the term means "to send down."

> We will recount to you the best of narratives in what We have revealed to you of this Qurʾan, and indeed prior to it you were among those who are unaware [of it]. (12:3)

This is the highest and the most sophisticated form of divine communication, and Muslims have always considered the Qurʾan as an instance of this phenomenon. According to Islamic beliefs, other divine books, such as the Torah, the Gospel, and the Psalms of Prophet David, are also examples of this connection between the Divinity and humankind.[8]

Some Aspects of Prophetic Revelation

To be able to be addressed directly by God and to receive His message and revelation requires a very high capacity. God is the most pure, and it is only the pure hearts that can fully grasp His message. It is said of Prophet Muhammad that "God has not sent any prophet [*nabiy*] or apostle [*rasūl*] unless he has completed his intellect and his intellect is superior to the intellects of his entire nation."[9]

Imam Hasan Askari, the eleventh Imam of the Shiʿa, is quoted as saying, "Verily, God found the heart of Muhammad the best and with the greatest capacity so He chose him for prophethood."[10]

The prophets are fully aware of the divine communication given them. Prophets who are recipients of *wahy* never doubt the veracity of what has been revealed to them. This is a very

[8] Commenting on the phrase "We revealed to them [the prophets] the performance of good deeds" in verse 21:73, ʿAllamah Tabatabaʾi asserts that one type of *wahy* is what he calls *tasdidiy*, i.e., the protective revelation that is identical with infallibility. This involves practical divine support for the person in order to perform good deeds. See *Al-Mizan*, vol. 1, pp. 274 and 284; vol. 5, p. 80; vol. 6, p. 261; vol. 10, p. 223; vol. 14, p. 305; and vol. 15, p. 286.

[9] *Usul al-Kafi*, vol. 1, p. 13.

[10] *Bihar al-Anwar*, vol. 18, p. 205.

important aspect of the Shiʿa doctrine of revelation. There is no particular disagreement among Muslims about the meaning of the revelation. The main distinction to be found in the writings of the Shiʿa scholars is ontological and epistemological. For example, basing themselves on rational and scriptural arguments, the Shiʿa reject any story suggesting that Prophet Muhammad or any other prophet had ever been in doubt about his mission. For prophets to doubt whether they are true prophets and then to be reassured by someone else is totally inconsistent with their being divinely appointed guides for the people. If a prophet himself is in doubt about his mission and message, how can people be expected to believe in him, to follow him wholeheartedly, and to sacrifice their lives and possessions in the way that he asks them?

The Qurʾan speaks of revelation as a kind of vision that accepts no illusion or error and cannot be disputed. For example, after talking about the incident of the ascension (*miʿraj*), the Qurʾan goes on to say,

> The heart did not deny what it saw. Will you then dispute with him about what he saw? Certainly he saw it yet another time, by the Lote Tree of the Ultimate Boundary, near which is the Garden of the Abode, when there covered the Lote Tree what covered it. The gaze did not swerve, nor did it overstep the bounds. Certainly he saw some of the greatest signs of his Lord. (53:11-18)

Zurarah, a well-known and trusted companion of Imam Sadiq, the sixth Imam, asked him how the Prophet became certain that it was a genuine revelation that he received and not a satanic temptation. Imam replied, "Verily when God chooses a servant of His to become an apostle [*rasūl*] He bestows upon that person confidence and tranquillity so what comes to him from God is like what he sees with his eyes."[11]

[11] Ibid., p. 262, and *Tafsiral-ʿAyyashi*, vol. 2, p. 201.

Once Imam Sadiq was asked how the Apostles (*rusul*, pl. of *rasūl*) knew that they were Apostles. Imam replied, "The veil [*ghita*] was removed from them."[12] Muhammad b. Muslim, another reliable narrator, says that he had a conversation with Imam Sadiq about *muhaddath* (literally, "the one to whom speech is made"). Imam said, "He hears the voice and does not see." Muhammad b. Muslim asked Imam, "[In that case,] how does he know that this was the speech of the angel?" Imam replied, "He will be bestowed with confidence and tranquillity so that he knows that it was the angel [that spoke to him]."[13]

Thus, one should not compare the knowledge that the prophets receive through revelation to the ordinary type of knowledge that human beings have, which is subject to change and doubt.

Though receiving divine revelation is an extraordinary gift, it should by no means be taken as a strange, dubious, or suspicious phenomenon. The Qur᾽an says,

> Does it seem odd to these people that We have revealed to a man from among themselves, [declaring], "Warn mankind, and give good news to the faithful that they are in good standing with their Lord?" The faithless say, "This is indeed a plain magician." (10:2)

In the course of human history there have been many prophets to whom God sent His *wahy*. The first prophet was Adam and the last was Muhammad, the Seal of the Prophets (33:40). The Qur᾽an says,

> We have revealed to you as We revealed to Noah and the Prophets after him; and We revealed to Abraham, Ishmael, Isaac, Jacob, the Tribes, Jesus, Job, Jonah, Aaron and Solomon and to David We gave the Psalms. Of some Apostles, We have already told you their story; of others We have not; and to Moses God spoke direct. [These are] Apostles who gave good news as well as warning that mankind after (the coming) of the Apostles

[12] *Bihar al-Anwar*, vol. 2, p. 205, and vol. 11, p. 56.

[13] Ibid., vol. 26, p. 68.

should have no plea against God: for God is exalted in power and wise. (4:163-65)[14]

Altogether, the Qur'an mentions twenty-five of the prophets and states that there were many more (40:78). Through the indications of hadiths, Muslims believe that there have been 124,000 prophets. Among them, Noah, Abraham, Moses, Jesus, and Muhammad are the most outstanding. These are called *Ulū al-ʿAzm*, meaning "those of great determination."

All the prophets were recipients of divine revelation. The Qur'an says, "We did not send [any apostles] before you except as men to whom We revealed" (12:109). However, this does not mean that all the prophets were given books. In addition to itself, the Qur'an speaks of four heavenly books: the Book of Abraham (87:19), the Psalms of David (4:163; 17:55), the Torah of Moses (2:87; 3:3, 4; 6:91, 154), and the Gospel of Jesus (5:46). This does not necessarily mean that there were no other books, but certainly there were many prophets who were not given books but were preaching the book of a previous prophet.

There is a consistency and homogeny in the message given to the prophets. Muslims believe that the harmony and consistency present in the divine creation extends to God's revelations. Divine messages communicated to the people through His messengers are to be harmonious too. If they are revealed by the same God to the same recipients (human beings), who have the same nature and genuine needs, in order to show them the path toward the maximum possible happiness and salvation, they

[14] Commenting on these verses, A Yusuf Ali says, "The list here given is in three groups. (1) The first group, Abraham's family, is the same as in ii. 136, (where see the note) and in iii. 84. (2) Then we have the prophets Jesus, Job and Jonah, who symbolise patience and perseverance. (3) Then we have Aaron the priest and Solomon the King, both great figures, but each subordinate to another primary figure, viz., Moses (mentioned in the next verse) and David (mentioned at the end of this verse). David's distinction was the Psalms, some of which are still extant." Abdullah Yusuf Ali, *The Holy Qur'an: Text, Translation and Commentary* (Elmhurst, NY: Tahrike Tarsile Qur'an, Inc., 2001 [1934]), p. 232. For an online version, see http://www.quran4u.com/Tafsiraya/Index.htm.

must be similar in nature. Of course, depending on varying conditions and factors, some details may be changed.

Thus, Muslims confirm and believe in all the prophets and consider all believers in God to be members of the same community of faith:

> The Apostle has faith in what has been sent down to him from his Lord, and all the faithful. Each [of them] has faith in Allah, His angels, His scriptures and His apostles. [They declare,] "We make no distinction between any of His apostles." And they say, "We hear and obey. Our Lord, forgive us, and toward You is the return." (2:285)

The various ways in which the prophets received divine communication can be understood from the following passage of the Qur'an:

> It is not [possible] for any human that Allah should speak to him except through revelation or from behind a curtain, or send a messenger who reveals by His permission whatever He wishes. Indeed He is all-exalted, all-wise. Thus have We revealed to you the Spirit of Our dispensation. You did not know what the Book is, nor what is faith; but We made it a light that We may guide by its means whomever We wish of Our servants. (42:51-52)

Based on these verses and Islamic narrations, Muslim scholars have distinguished between three different methods of divine communication to the prophets:

1. *Direct and immediate communication.* This is interpreted to be of two kinds:
   a. A suggestion thrown by God into the heart or mind of a prophet, by which he understands the substance of the message, whether it is a command or prohibition or an explanation of a great truth.
   b. Verbal or literal communication, by which the actual words of God are conveyed in human language.

2. *From behind a veil.* This is not, of course, a material veil but the veil of Light.[15] In this sort of communication, the prophet hears a voice but does not see the one to whom the voice belongs. This has been likened to hearing the voice of a person from behind a curtain. Prophet Moses received the revelation from God on Mount Sinai in this way. So did Prophet Muhammad in the Night of Miʿraj.[16]

3. *By sending a messenger (rasūl).* This messenger was the angel Gabriel, through whom the revelations were given to the Holy Prophet. Prophet Muhammad usually received the revelations in this way. The Qurʾan says:

> This is indeed [a Book] sent down by the Lord of all the worlds, brought down by the Trustworthy Spirit upon your heart . . . in a clear Arabic language. (26:192-95)
>
> Say [O Muhammad, to mankind], "Whoever is an enemy of Gabriel [should know that] it is he who has brought it down on your heart with the will of Allah, confirming what has been [revealed] before it, and as a guidance and good news to the faithful. (2:97)

It has been suggested that revelation by sending a messenger takes one of the following forms:

1. The angel deposits the revelation in the spirit of the prophets without appearing to them.

2. The angel appears as a human being and speaks to the prophets. For example, there are historical reports that on occasion Gabriel appeared to Prophet Muhammad in the

[15] There is a tradition that the Prophet said, "His veil is Light: were He to withdraw it, then would the august splendours of His countenance surely consume everything that comes within His Sight." *Sahih* of Muslim, section on Imaan; *Musnad* of Ahmad ibn Hanbal, vol. 4, pp. 401 and 405; introduction to *Sunan* of Ibn Majah, p. 13.

[16] Ayatollah M H Maʾrifat, *ʿUlum-e Qurʾani*, p. 25.

form of Dehyah al-Kalbi, who was the foster brother of the Prophet.

3. The angel speaks in the ears of the prophets like a bell. This was the most difficult type of the revelation.
4. Gabriel appears for the Prophet in the same form that God has created him.[17]

The above relate to the ways and styles of revelation to the prophets. What was actually revealed to the prophets (i.e., the content of the revelations) will be studied below.

Muslims believe in the immunity of the Qur'an on historical grounds and on the basis of its being protected by God:

> Indeed We have sent down the Reminder [the Qur'an], and indeed We will preserve it. (15:9)
>
> Indeed it [the Qur'an] is an august Book: falsehood cannot approach it, from before it nor from behind it, a [gradually] sent down [revelation] from One all-wise, all-laudable. (41:41-42)

The message originates from divine knowledge, so it must be true and completely pure: "But Allah bears witness to what He has sent down to you—He sent it down with His knowledge—and the angels bear witness [too], and Allah quite suffices as a witness" (4:166).

The messenger who brings down the message, Gabriel, is trusted, and so is the recipient who acts as a messenger to human beings. Prophet Muhammad has a passive role in this regard; that is, he does not add anything of his personality to what has been revealed. He only acts as a pure and clean channel.[18] The

[17] *Al-Mizan*, vol. 18, p. 74; *Tafsir Nemuneh*, vol. 20, p. 488.

[18] This idea is also clearly mentioned in the hadiths of the Prophet and of his household. E.g., arguing for the need for the prophethood and revelation from God, Imam Rida argues that there was a need to appoint infallible (*ma'sum*) apostles to convey divine commands and prohibitions and etiquettes to the people and to inform them about what benefits them or harms them, since they could not understand these by themselves (*Bihar al-Anwar*, vol. 11, p. 40).

Qur᾽an clearly rejects any possibility of something being added to the Qur᾽an by the Prophet:

> Had he faked any sayings in Our name, We would have surely seized him by the right hand and then cut off his aorta, and none of you could have held Us off from him. Indeed it is a reminder for the Godwary. Indeed We know that there are some among you who deny [it]. And indeed it will be a [matter of] regret for the faithless. It is indeed certain truth. So celebrate the Name of your Lord, the All-supreme. (69:44-52)

In the case of the Qur᾽an, the revelation certainly included actual wording. In this regard, ʿAllamah Tabataba᾽i writes:

> The general belief of Muslims concerning the revelation, based on the Qur᾽an, is that the text of the Qur᾽an is the actual speech of God transmitted to the Prophet by one of His chosen angels.
>
> The name of this angel, or heavenly being, is Gabriel or the Faithful Spirit. He transmitted the word of God over a period of twenty-three years to the Prophet. He would bring the divine instructions to the Prophet, who would relate them faithfully to the people using the same words in the form of a verse.[19]

As indicated above, the main reason for such belief is the Qur᾽an itself. What follows are different types of evidence for this idea from the Qur᾽an and from various hadiths to further support it.

With respect to the Qur᾽anic verses, reference should predominantly be made to those verses in which the Qur᾽an is described or to the verbs that indicate the way in which the Qur᾽an is or should be treated. Regarding the former, the following are titles to which the Qur᾽an may be referred:

1. *Qur᾽an.* The term *Qur᾽an* literally means "something that is readable." Thus, it must consist of words. In the first instance of divine revelation to the Prophet, he was told, "Read in the Name of your Lord who created. . . . Read, and your Lord is the most generous, who taught by the pen"

[19] *The Qur᾽an in Islam*, part III.

(96:1, 3-4). This shows that what was revealed was a scripture that could be read. Though in Arabic *qa-ra-ʿa* includes reading or reciting by heart, it is only applicable when a text or script is involved.

2. *Kitāb* (book) or its cognates. For example, *"Alif, Lam, Ra.* [This is] a Book, whose signs have been made definitive and then elaborated, from One [who is] all-wise, all-aware" (11:1).[20]
3. *Suhuf* (pages; scriptures). The Qurʾan says, "An apostle from Allah reciting impeccable scriptures" (98:2, 3).
4. *Kalāmullāh* (Word or Speech of God). For example, "If any of the polytheists seeks asylum from you, grant him asylum until he hears the Word of Allah. Then convey him to his place of safety. That is because they are a people who do not know" (9:6).
5. *Qawl* (speech). The Qurʾan says, "Indeed soon We shall cast on you a weighty word" (73:5).

Regarding the latter—that is, the verbs that indicate the way in which the Qurʾan is or should be treated—the following verses can be referred to:

1. *Qiraaʾah* and its cognates. For example, God says, "And when We have recited it, follow its recitation" (75:18).
2. *Tilāwah* and its cognates. For example, God says in the Qurʾan, "These are the signs of God which We recite for you in truth, and *you* are indeed one of the apostles" (2:252; emphasis added).
3. *Tartil* and its cognates. The Prophet was told, "Recite the Qurʾan in a measured tone" (73:4). Not only was Prophet Muhammad supposed to recite the Qurʾan in a measured

[20] See also the verses 32:2-3 and 40:2. "The revelation of this Book is from God Exalted in Power Full of Knowledge" (40:2).

tone, but also God the Almighty says that in the first place He Himself has recited the Qurʾan to the Prophet in a measured tone: "The faithless say, 'Why has not the Qurʾan been sent down to him all at once?' So it is, that We may strengthen *your* heart with it, and We have recited it [to you] in a measured tone" (25:32).

Furthermore, it is a recognized fact that the Qurʾan was revealed in Arabic. If the revelation did not include the actual wordings of the Qurʾan, there would be no place for discussions about its language. For example, the Qurʾan says,

> This is indeed [a Book] sent down by the Lord of all the worlds, brought down by the Trustworthy Spirit upon your heart . . . in a clear Arabic language. (26:192-95)

> Yet before it the Book of Moses was a guide and a mercy, and this is a Book which confirms it, in the Arabic language, to warn those who do wrong, and is a [bearer of] good news for the virtuous. (46:12)

In addition to Qurʾanic evidence, one may also refer to the numerous hadiths in which the same titles or verbs are used for the Qurʾan. For example, Imam Ali says, "Verily, God . . . sent down to him [Prophet Muhammad] the book with truth."[21] This is why Muslims believe that translations of the Qurʾan, however accurate and perfect they may be, are just translations and can by no means be considered to be the Qurʾan itself. It should also be noted that the hadiths of Prophet Muhammad, despite their eloquence and profound meanings, are completely different and distinct from the Qurʾanic verses; anyone familiar with the Arabic language can verify this. This, by itself, is another piece of evidence for the idea that the wording of the Qurʾan is not from the Prophet.

[21] *Bihar al-Anwar*, vol. 92, p. 81.

Therefore, the Muslim understanding of the Qur'an is that it was revealed by God to the Prophet with the exact wording that has always been there and that is still there today.[22]

The Qur'an has been revealed in clear and plain language so that the people can understand it and take benefit from it. In addition to the above verses, we read in the Qur'an, "Certainly We have made the Qur'an simple for the sake of admonishment." This verse is repeated four times in the same chapter (54:17, 22, 32, 40). The Qur'an also says:

> Indeed We have made it simple in your language, so that they may take admonition. (44:58)
>
> Certainly we have drawn for mankind in this Qur'an every [kind of] example, so that they may take admonition—an Arabic Qur'an, without any deviousness, so that they may be Godwary. (39:27, 28)

There are deeper layers of the meaning of the Qur'an for which extra guidance from the Qur'an or the *Sunnah* is required. This is where the process of *tafsir* is involved. *Tafsir* is a profound Arabic term. Literally, it means to "uncover" or to "unveil." Technically, it means to clarify and explain the hidden or concealed aspects of a text. Sometimes a text may convey different possibilities or alternative meanings. Therefore, it would need an act of interpretation, or *tafsir*, to define what is really meant by the speaker or the writer. Sometimes a text has a clear and apparent meaning, but there might be some more fundamental or underlying levels of meaning. Here *tafsir* would involve an act of unveiling and exposing those inner meanings.[23]

[22] For the statements of the Shiʿa scholars in this regard, see *Shiʿi Islam: Origins, Faith and Practices*, pp. 32–35.

[23] Therefore, the real task of *tafsir* starts just after defining the following: the lexical meaning (this is deduced from the root of the word), the morphological meaning (this is deduced from the structure of the word), and the grammatical meaning (this is deduced from the function and position of the word with respect to the whole speech).

A sound *tafsir* can never be in conflict with the outer meaning.[24] Moreover, a sound *tafsir* has to be able to show the relationship between the apparent or outer meaning and the underlying or inner meaning. In other words, an acceptable *tafsir* is the one that is able to show how the outer meaning refers to the inner meaning and how the inner meaning, in turn, refers back to the outer meaning. This is why another title for *tafsir* among the early exegetes of the Qurʾan—like Abu Jaʾfar al-Tabari in *Jaamiʾ al-Bayaan*—was *taʾwil*, which literally means "to refer."[25]

The first person to interpret the Qurʾan was Prophet Muhammad. According to the Qurʾan itself, the task of the Prophet was to recite the Qurʾan for the people, to teach and explain it to them, and to put it into practice so that he could be taken as an example for those who want to follow the Qurʾan and to implement its teaching and value system in society.[26] Therefore, to teach and to explain the Qurʾan involved more than just reciting the Qurʾan to the Arabs who were themselves able to understand the literal meaning of it.

According to the well-known hadith of *thaqalayn* and other hadiths, the Prophet has given the responsibility of interpreting the Qurʾan to his household.[27] Among the household of the

[24] In his preface to *Al-Mizan*, ʿAllamah Tabatabaʾi writes, "As a direct result of this method, we have never felt any need to interpret a verse against its apparent meaning. As we have said earlier, this type of interpretation is in fact misinterpretation."

[25] It has to be noted that *taʾwil* is used in different ways. For a comprehensive discussion on this issue, see *Al-Tafsir wa al-Mufassirun*, vol. 1. ʿAllamah Tabatabʾi has a special idea about *taʾwil*, in which he basically takes *taʾwil* to mean the reality to which the text refers. For his view on *taʾwil*, see, e.g., *Al-Mizan*, vol. 2, p. 14; vol. 3, pp. 49–53; and vol. 13, p. 376.

[26] E.g., refer to the beginning of chapter Friday and verse 44 of chapter The Bee.

[27] The hadith of *Thaqalayn* has been narrated in major sources of all schools of Islam. This tradition was uttered by the Prophet on different occasions, including the day of ʿArafah in his last pilgrimage and the eighteenth of *Dhuʾl-Hijjah* in Ghadir Khum. Despite minor differences in the wording, the essence remains the same in all versions of the tradition. e.g., in one

Prophet the first to interpret the Qur᾿an and introduce the Qur᾿anic teachings to Muslims was Ali b. Abi Talib, the cousin and son-in-law of the Prophet who was brought up in the house of the Prophet.

---

version of the hadith the Prophet is quoted as saying, "Oh people! I leave among you two precious things: the Book of God and my household. As long as you hold on to them you will not go astray."

For different versions of this hadith and its sources and interpretation, see M. A. Shomali, *Shiʿi Islam: Origins, Faith and Practices* (London: Islamic College for Advanced Studies, 2001).

Chapter 2

Lectio Divina

A Monastic Perspective on *Lectio Divina*

Guido Dotti

In the Western Christian tradition the Latin term *lectio divina*—literally, "divine reading"—means the prayerful reading, usually by oneself, of the Holy Scriptures, sometimes accompanied by texts of the church fathers. It has for its aim knowledge of God, a personal relation with God, and transformation of one's own life according to the image of Jesus Christ, the living Word of God.

The expression is already found in Origen (third century), who speaks of *theia anagnosis*.[1] Eventually, *lectio divina* will come to indicate the practice of personal meditation on Scripture, which, united with spiritual struggle, flows into prayer.

[1] Origen, *Epistula ad Gregorium Thaumaturgum* 4, Sources Chrétiennes 148 (Paris: Éditions du Cerf, 1969), p. 192.

Beyond the various forms that it will assume over the centuries in the spiritual practice of the Christian West, it is not so much a "method" of reading Scripture or one "observance" among many, but rather an interior disposition. Christians believe that we are each invited by the Holy Spirit to approach the Word of God proclaimed in public worship in such a way that we may assimilate it as a word addressed to us in the precise conditions of our actual lives.

The Word of God for the Community of Believers and for Each Individual

Holy Scripture is, in fact, script—a text *written* under the inspiration of the Holy Spirit to be read aloud to a believing community that has been called together by the Word to listen to this Divine Word and then to put it into practice. These dynamics of calling, assembling, listening, and responding are already present in the Hebrew tradition,[2] that which grew up both around the temple of Jerusalem and later around the synagogue. Two examples are found in the Bible itself. In Nehemiah 8:1-12 we have the account of the proclamation of the entire Torah before all the people assembled in Jerusalem, while in Luke 4:12-22 we have a description of Jesus participating in a synagogue liturgy in Nazareth, where he reads from the scroll of the prophet Isaiah and then comments on it.

This Word that molds the community as a whole is also meant to mold individual believers by becoming God's Word for them here and now. It is here that the personal relation of the individual Christian with the Word of God assumes its full importance. After listening to the proclamation of the Word during the community liturgy, the Christian is called upon to receive it in his own heart and in his own mind, to "ruminate" on it in order to assimilate its spiritual substance.

In the predominantly oral culture of Christianity's first centuries, the memorization of biblical texts was a common way of

[2] Later on we find them also in Islam.

learning the Scriptures. The monks of the Egyptian desert, for the most part illiterate, were required to learn "by heart some Scripture: at least the New Testament and the Psalter," so as to be able to recall it to mind and repeat it in a low voice throughout the day.[3] Still today, just as then, an elder may give a disciple a simple verse of Scripture that is to be repeated continually until it becomes "second nature," an integral part of one's own thought and action. Then another word to be recalled and lived is given and received.

What Is Sacred Scripture and How Does One Interpret It?

Three fundamental convictions, which go back to the patristic age, seem to me to be decisive to grasp the significance of the practice of *lectio divina* today.

First of all, Saint Jerome (fourth century) affirms, and the Second Vatican Council repeats, that "Sacred Scripture is to be read and interpreted with the aid of the same Spirit through which it was written."[4]

Second, there is the conviction that the Bible, although composed of many books—the Greek term *biblia*, in fact, means "books"—is in reality one book containing the Word of God that narrates, in many different ways, the one account of God's love for humankind. This means that *Scriptura suae ipsius interpres* (Scripture is its own interpreter), that is, that every single passage or book of the Bible is to be read and interpreted in the light of other biblical passages in order to grasp its deepest and unifying meaning. In this effort of interpretation the inspiration of the Holy Spirit, as mentioned above, is fundamental, for the

[3] Pachomius, *Precepts* 140, in *Pachomian koinonia*, vol. 2, ed. Armand Veilleux (Kalamazoo, MI: Cistercian Publications, 1981), p. 166.

[4] See *Dei Verbum* 12. The Conciliar document refers to Saint Jerome's commentary on Galatians (5:19-20) and indicates that this quotation can be found in Migne's *Patrologia Latina*, vol. 26, column 417A. The column reference seems to be in error; it should probably be 445A.

Spirit guides the church, the community of believers in every time and in every place, so that it may be ever faithful to the intention of the divine Legislator. In this sense we can take up another patristic adage, which is often attributed to Gregory the Great: *Scriptura crescit cum legente* (Scripture grows with the one who reads it); that is, it acquires new and richer meanings, which in turn increase the spiritual stature of those who regularly approach it.

Finally, there is the conviction that every passage of Sacred Scripture, including those of the Old Testament, speaks of Jesus Christ, the Word made flesh. As a consequence, "ignorance of Scripture is ignorance of Christ."[5] It is Christ whom the faithful should seek in the story of the people of Israel, in the precepts of the Law, in the words of the Prophets. The evangelist Luke makes this clear at the end of his gospel, when the risen Christ appears to two disciples on their way to Emmaus and tells them, " 'Was it not necessary that the Messiah should suffer these things and then enter into his glory?' Then beginning with Moses and all the prophets, he interpreted to them the things about himself in all the scriptures" (Luke 24:26–27).

The Rule of Saint Benedict and *Lectio Divina*

If these are the basic convictions that animate and motivate *lectio divina*, its practice, as it has been taken up again in the Catholic Church in the last fifty years, has its roots in the Rule of Saint Benedict.[6] Although this Rule, written by Benedict of Nursia (present-day Norcia) in the sixth century and, in the ninth century, mandated as the rule to be followed in all monasteries of the Holy Roman Empire, does not describe a method or even

[5] Jerome, *Commentary on Isaiah*, prologue, *Corpus Christianorum Series Latina* 73, 73A.

[6] See "*Lectio divina* et lecture spirituelle," *Dictionnaire de spiritualité*, 9 (1976): 470–510; Enzo Bianchi, *Praying the Word: An Introduction to* Lectio Divina (Kalamazoo, MI: Cistercian, 1998).

spell out the profound spiritual motivations for doing *lectio divina,* this practice became the characteristic patrimony of monks living under Benedict's Rule. While it contains no chapter that has *lectio divina* for its title or exclusive topic, we can find precious indications throughout the Rule regarding its practice.

The *object* of *lectio* is fundamentally Sacred Scripture as it is proclaimed in the Divine Office, the community prayer that calls together the monks seven times a day. To this can be added patristic texts and commentaries, which, incidentally, were themselves largely composed of scriptural references. At the beginning of Lent, every monk received a codex of the Bible, which he was to read "the whole of it straight through" (RB 48.15). This disposition continued the Hebrew tradition of *lectio cursiva,* the continuous reading from beginning to end, of the biblical text. (We see a similar tradition in the reading of the Qur'an during Ramadan.) In the communal proclamation and still more in personal reading one does not take a text at random or jump from one book to another; rather, one follows a precise order without omitting anything.

The Rule of Saint Benedict also determines the *times* that are to be dedicated to *lectio* during the day. It is scheduled for the hours that were least fit for manual work: the hottest in summer and the darkest in winter.

The *aim* of *lectio,* for Saint Benedict, is to render Scripture familiar to the monk, leading him from the repetitive murmuring of a biblical phrase or verse to the point where it "inhabits" his silence. The final goal is that the monk should arrive at an ever-deeper knowledge of Christ and put into practice the Word listened to and prayed.

The Four Steps of the Spiritual Ladder

From these simple, but fundamental, indications, the medieval monastic tradition succeeded in furnishing a real and true "guide" to *lectio divina.* In a twelfth-century letter to his friend Gervase on the contemplative life, Guigo II, prior of the Grande

Chartreuse, sets out in detail the various moments of *lectio* as a practice of personal prayer. It indicates that there are four steps on this spiritual ladder: *lectio, meditatio, oratio, contemplatio* (reading, meditation, prayer, contemplation). We will now analyze each of these steps in greater detail, beginning with some preliminaries.[7]

1. Before beginning *lectio,* it is necessary to create a space of silence in which the Word can sound with all its force without being suffocated by voices and preoccupations that are foreign to it. Then, with a simple prayer, we invoke the Holy Spirit, who opens the ears of the heart and predisposes us to listen and to enter into a loving dialogue with the Lord.

2. *Lectio divina* means "divine reading," that is, the act of reading an inspired text that is not chosen by the individual believer at random but is received from the church either through its proclamation in communal prayer or from a lectionary that indicates which passages of Scripture are to be read each day. Reading means proceeding calmly and attentively, as if coming to the text for the first time, perhaps with the help of various expedients that permit one to enter deeply into the text so as to grasp its genuine meaning. For example, one can read it aloud, repeat the text without looking at it, copy some phrases, or read the text in other versions: the original language, a translation other than that which is most familiar, or a modern language different from one's own.

3. *Meditatio* (meditation) is not introspective reflection or a kind of psychological self-analysis, but rather a close examination of the passage read. To this end it is also possible to make use of studies and commentaries, specifically those that aim to bridge the cultural distance that separates us from the Bible. This "meditation" helps us discover its

[7] See Guigo II, *The Ladder of Monks and Twelve Meditations,* trans. Edmond College and James Walsh (Kalamazoo, MI: Cistercian, 1981).

central point, the key verse of the text, which could then be repeated during the rest of the day. In this way a "dialogue" is initiated between the text and the person who reads, an exchange between the reader's life and the contents of the text through which, as was mentioned above, both the Scriptures and the person reading them "grow."

4. *Oratio* (prayer) then flows into a dialogue in which the believer senses that he or she is directly addressed by God and answers Him with the "you" of loving confidence. This prayer, which the Spirit adapts to each one in a very personal manner, can assume all the shadings that prayer knows with the change of events and of life's seasons: supplication, invocation, praise, thanksgiving, intercession, adoring silence, tears of repentance.
5. Finally, *contemplatio* (contemplation) is the step about which the least can be said. It is a deeply personal experience that remains almost indescribable. Fundamentally, the Christian contemplation that comes from *lectio divina* is not "seeing" God, whom no living being could ever see except as reflected in the face of the Son of God, but rather "contemplating" oneself, others, and the world with God's eyes, seeing these as God Himself sees them.

In this sense, the most meaningful description I have found of authentic Christian contemplation that is born of *lectio divina* is in two monastic texts, one ancient, the other contemporary. The first is found in the *Dialogues* of Gregory the Great, who, describing the life of Saint Benedict, attests that one day, "the whole world, gathered together as it were under one beam of the sun, was presented before his eyes."[8] The second is a passage in the testament of Christian de Chergé, the prior of Tibhirine, a Cistercian monastery in Algeria, who in March 1996 was abducted and killed together with six of his brothers. This is how he writes of the ardent desire that had inhabited his life, which

[8] Gregory the Great, *Dialogues* II, 35.

was spent in a fraternal dialogue with Muslims, and of the moment of his death, which he sensed might well come through an act of violence:

> My avid curiosity will then be satisfied. This is what I shall be able to do, if God wills—immerse my gaze in that of the Father, and contemplate with him his children of Islam just as he sees them, all shining with the glory of Christ, the fruit of His Passion, and filled with the Gift of the Spirit, whose secret joy will always be to establish communion and to refashion the likeness, playfully delighting in the differences.[9]

In view of the context in which I speak, my reflection might end here.

I prefer, however, to end by saying that the practice of *lectio divina*, after an "exile" from church life and even from monasticism that lasted for centuries, has returned to the heart of Christian spiritual life and has passed beyond monastery walls, becoming familiar to very many Christian faithful. Not by chance does Pope Benedict XVI, in the document edited after the synod of bishops dedicated to the Word of God (2010), write:

> The Synod frequently insisted on the need for a prayerful approach to the sacred text as a fundamental element in the spiritual life of every believer, in the various ministries and states in life, with particular reference to *lectio divina* . . ., which is truly "capable of opening up to the faithful the treasures of God's word, but also of bringing about an encounter with Christ, the living word of God."[10]

[9] Christian de Chergé, "Testament," *Monastic Interreligious Dialogue Bulletin* 55 (May 1996); English translation available online at http://monasticdialog.com/a.php?id=497.

[10] Benedict XVI, post-synodal apostolic exhortation *Verbum Domini*, nos. 86–87, www.vatican.va/holy_father/benedict_xvi/apost_exhortations/documents/hf_ben-xvi_exh_20100930_verbum-domini_en.html#The_Word_Of_God_In_The_Life_Of_The_Church.

A Shiʿite Perspective on *Lectio Divina*

Farrokh Sekaleshfar

> *There is indeed an admonition in that for one who has a heart, or gives ear, being attentive.* (50:37)
>
> *Allah manifests Himself through His Book; however, you do not see.*
> —Imam Sadiq[1]

When describing the philosophy behind creation, Allah indirectly answers the question by saying, "I did not create the jinn and the humans except that they worship Me" (51:56). Imam Sadiq defines worshiping as being on a par with "knowing Him."[2] This genre of knowing, however, does not refer to an imaginative, philosophical, academic, or rational exercise. The reality of this "knowing" is *seeing* Allah and ultimately *being* Allah-like. This *seeing* and *becoming* has been touched upon by the verses of the Holy Qurʾan and traditions of the Ahl al-Bayt. Imam Ali states,

> Verily with Allah is a drink for His friends, whenever they drink it, they become intoxicated; when they become intoxicated, they become ecstatic; on becoming ecstatic, they become purified

[1] M. B. Majlisi, *Bihar al-Anwar* (Ocean of lights) (Beirut: Dār Ihyāʾ al-Turāth al-Arabī Publications, 1983), vol. 89:107.

[2] M. H. Tabatabai, *Al-Mizan* (The Balance: Commentary of the Holy Qurʾan) (Beirut: Dār Ihyāʾ al-Turāth al-Arabī Publications, 2006), vol. 18:390.

> [from impurities]; on becoming purified, they melt; on melting they become sincere; on becoming sincere, they become made sincere; after being made sincere, they seek and on seeking they will find and on finding, they join and it is on joining that they attain unity [with Allah]. *There is no difference between them and their Beloved.*[3]

In 76:5-6 Allah states, "Indeed the pious will drink from a cup seasoned with camphor, a spring where the servants of Allah drink, which they make to gush forth as they please." In 83:25-28 one reads concerning the pious, "You will perceive in their faces the freshness of bliss as they are served with a sealed wine whose seal is musk—for such let the viers vie—and whose seasoning is from *tasnim*, a spring where those brought near [to Allah] drink." In 76:21 He states, "Their Lord will give them to drink a pure drink." Concerning this pure drink, Imam Sadiq said, "This heavenly drink is one which cleanses someone from other than Allah [*ma siwallah*]."[4] Note that the drink is in heaven but must be drunk here on earth in order for it to be manifested in heaven. Whatever perfection resides in heaven is transferred there via you (i.e., the immaterial rational spirit) from this world. In short, all perfections are *iktisābi* (earned) and *intiqāli* (conveyed). This world is but a farm for the Hereafter, but this farm is everything; it is the soul. It is you! Perfection emanates from within; one cannot acquire it from people, books, religious icons, and so on.

This gnosis of Allah, therefore, is the ultimate objective. Anything less is tantamount to imperfection. This is the potential we, as humans, possess. Only on fruition and realization will perfection qualify. One of the routes and methods of attaining to this lofty goal is that of *lectio divina* (divine reading) or, in

[3] S. H. Amuli (d. 782 AH), *Al-Bahr al-Aʾẓam* (Esoteric exegesis of the Holy Qurʾan) (Qum: ʿAl-Mahdi al-thaqāfī Nūrun ʿalā Nūrʾ Publications, 2010), vol. 1:266. Emphasis added.

[4] M. F. Kashani, *Tafsir al-Safi* (Beirut: Al-ʿAlami Institute Publications, 1991), vol. 5:265.

Islamic terms, reciting the Qurʾan (lit. *lectio*). Naturally, merely reading the scripture will never suffice in relation to attaining to unity with Allah (communion), although it is a necessary first step. The essentially pivotal criterion required on behalf of the wayfarer to Allah is observing the process of *murāqabah* (self-scrutiny). *Murāqabah* is the key to this unity and annihilation (*fanāʾ*) with respect to Allah. *Murāqabah* is the key to divine dreams; *murāqabah* is the key to visions while awake; *murāqabah* is the key to experiencing what the Greeks referred to as "Hades" (*barzakh*), as well as heaven, hell, and even Resurrection (*Qiyāmah*) in this world. In short, *murāqabah* is a tool for transcending all metaphysical realms of existences until one becomes annihilated in Allah's essence (like a wave in the ocean). *Murāqabah* enables the heart to contemplate actively and consciously the sole, true One existent (Allah), converting our transient awareness into true prayer and remembrance of God.

In what follows, I will outline the conditions one needs to complete before embarking on the route of *murāqabah*—including the mannerisms and etiquette involved in reciting scripture. I shall then demonstrate the process of *murāqabah* itself and finally describe some results and "visions of communion" experienced by well-known spiritual wayfarers.

Preliminary Requirements before Initiating *Murāqabah*

The primary concern for the traveler on the journey to Allah is that of acquiring *taqwa*, which here signifies the spiritual disposition by means of which one refrains from sins and executes all obligatory actions. This state of the spirit must be enhanced and strengthened to such a degree that *taqwa* becomes second nature (*malakah*) to the person. The possession of this caliber of *taqwa* is not perfection per se; it is merely a means to perfection. One with *taqwa* (*muttaqī*) may even acquire heaven in the Hereafter, but one's potential is much more. Heaven at this stage is merely recreational. One may be *muttaqī*, as defined above, but lack numerous ethical and gnostic stations and qualities (e.g., one may be suffering from jealousy or occupied with a materialistic life). *Taqwa*, as defined above, is only a preliminary measure that is necessary but not sufficient.

Role and Etiquette of Reciting

The Qurʾan is the verbal, and thus physical, manifestation of Allah's attributes; it is a "worldly" reflection of an ultimately complex truth not attainable in its entirety. The importance of scripture is highlighted by the fact that its recitation acts as a starting point for acquiring access to the speaker, that is, Allah. The Holy Qurʾan possesses over six thousand verses, each of which has an external, *prima facie* meaning. More importantly, we have been told by the Imams that each verse possesses up to seventy esoteric dimensions (*buṭūn*).[5] Even the esoteric dimensions have subdimensions within them. The ultimate esoteric dimension (*abṭan ul-bawaṭin*) is Allah Himself. Bursī, a well-known Shiʿa gnostic, quotes Allah as saying in the Bible, "Your external side is to be annihilated whilst your inner side [*bāṭinuka*] is I [*ana*]."[6] The more one transcends the realms of existences (such as the realms of "Hades" (*barzakh*), the angelic world, etc.), the more one will gain access to the metaphysical truths of the Holy Book, whose most lowly manifestation is the Arabic scripture we have in our hands today.

Due to the sacrosanct importance of what the Holy Book is reflecting, these very words are treated with utmost devotion and respect. The degree of devotion is so great that one is not allowed to touch them without being in a state of *wudu* (a ritual washing and wiping of specific limbs that permits one to carry out different actions, namely, touching the Qurʾanic script). Although being in a state of *wudu* is not a canonical prerequisite

[5] Ibid., 1:203.

[6] Ibid., 1:244.

to reciting (as it is to touching the script), the scholars of Gnosticism have enjoined the *wudu* before recitation. The reason for this is related to the supplications that accompany the washing or wiping of each limb. These supplications involve imploring Allah's assistance in purifying our hearts in addition to the actions of our limbs.

Etiquette of Recitation

The traditions describe a vast spectrum of physical and mental activities that aid the recitation of the Qurʾan in a way that makes it possible to reach one's ultimate destination. These include:

1. *Washing one's mouth before recitation.* Mouths have been described in prophetic traditions as "transits" to the Qurʾan. As the Holy Prophet said, "Freshen your mouths with a pleasant aroma; after all, your mouths are a transit to the Qurʾan."[7]
2. *Uttering the formula of "seeking protection"* (*istiʾāthah*; i.e., uttering the formula "I seek protection of Allah from the outcast Satan"). In 16:98 we read, "When you recite the Qurʾan, seek the protection of Allah against the outcast Satan." Imam Sadiq said that we should "lock the doors to sinning by means of uttering the formula of *istiʾāthah* and open the doors of obedience by reciting the *basmalah* formula."[8] (*Basmalah* refers to the formula "In the Name of Allah, the Universally Merciful, the Specifically Merciful.")
3. *Reciting in a measured tone.* In 73:4 we read, "Recite the Qurʾan in a measured tone." Commentating on this verse, the Holy Prophet said, "Recite the Qurʾan articulately and in a measured tone; do not execute it in a manner such as

[7] M. Reyshahri, compiler, *Al-Mizan al-Hikmah* (Compendium of Shiʿa traditions) (Qum: Dar al-Hadith Publications, 2004), vol. 10:4826.

[8] Ibid.

the random cultivation of seeds or the hurried reading of poems; pontificate over its marvels and synchronize your recitation with the heart's pulse and do not let your endeavors be confined to merely completing the chapter."[9]

4. *Deliberating/contemplating while reciting.* In 47:24 we read, "Do they not contemplate the Qur᾽an, or are there locks on the hearts?" And in 38:29 we read, "It is a blessed Book that We have sent down to you, so that they may contemplate its signs, and that those who possess intellect may take admonition." In 4:82 Allah states, "Do they not contemplate the Qur᾽an? Had it been from someone other than Allah, they would have surely found much discrepancy in it." Imam Ali said, "There is no virtue in recitation that is not accompanied by contemplation."[10] The Holy Prophet said, "Whoever completes the Qur᾽an's recitation within three days, will not acquire true understanding with respect to it."[11]

5. *Humility.* In 57:16 we read, "Is it not time yet for those who have faith that their hearts should be humbled for Allah's remembrance and to the truth which has come down to them, and not to be like those who were given the Book before [referring to the Jews]?" The Holy Prophet would always enjoin weeping and lamentation when reciting the Qur᾽an.

Murāqabah

After having completed these stages of *taqwa* and etiquette (or possibly even during this stage), one enters the stage of *murāqabah*, which involves the evolution of one's intention. Before this stage, the actions of one's limbs were controlled, but

[9] Ibid.

[10] Ibid.

[11] Ibid.

one's intentions were dormant and latent. However, from now on, the intention is activated in a particular manner. The more refined one's intentions become, the more purified one's spiritual development becomes. As the Holy Prophet said, "Actions are only based on [one's] intentions."[12] In *murāqabah* all one's actions must be scrutinized in accordance with a "filter" system. By entering one's actions into such a mechanism of intention, the output will be actions that are truly acceptable before Allah. Not undergoing this process leads one to carry out empty actions from morning to night. As we read in 29:64, "The worldly life is nothing but diversion and play."

Murāqabah comprises four broad stages or steps;[13] in other words, we are dealing with four paradigms of intention. In step one, before accomplishing or encountering any action, one must scrutinize and ask oneself, "Is this action canonically obligatory or prohibited?" By doing so, one is intensifying one's *taqwa* and solidifying one's spirit of abiding by the *shariah*. Assuming one succeeds with this dimension of step one, one may proceed with other dimensions, such as making sure one maximally executes *mustahabat* (canonically recommended actions) and maximally refrains from *makruhat* (canonically undesirable actions).

In step two of *murāqabah*, the filter mechanism becomes more difficult and delicate to execute. Here, before executing any given action, one must ask oneself whether or not one is acquiring Allah's pleasure by carrying out such an action. "Am I doing this action to please Allah irrespective of what the outcome is?" This is the key question in step two. Truly intending such an objective is very difficult. By way of example, when you help someone, will you be upset if he or she does not return or compensate your good deed? If so, then it becomes evident that Allah's pleasure was never truly intended. As one ethicist put

[12] M. B. Majlisi, Bihar al-Anwar (Ocean of lights) (Beirut: Dār Ihyāʾ al-Turāth al-Arabī Publications, 1983), vol. 67:111.

[13] M. H. H. Tehrani, *Treatise of the Kernel of Kernels* (Compilation of Allamah Tabatabai's lecture notes on spiritual wayfaring) (Qum: Allamah Tabatabai Publications, 2009), p. 144.

it, "You should reach a stage whereby even if you end in Hell, you still will not be prepared to exchange the action you had done for acquiring Allah's pleasure with anything else, including relief from punishment."[14] On succeeding with step two, one's sincerity (*ikhlāṣ*) before Allah becomes enhanced. Acquiring true sincerity (i.e., being a *mukhliṣ*) is the penultimate objective in the process of *murāqabah*. The main goal is yet to come.

Stages three and four are summarized in a prophetic tradition that states, "Worship Allah as if you see Him; and if you don't see Him, acknowledge that He sees you."[15] Step three means acknowledging that Allah sees you in all actions that you pursue. The final step means that every act you perform is done with the full awareness that He actually sees you in every moment.

All these steps aim to purify one's sincerity before Allah, paving the way to seeing Him in actuality (with the eyes of the heart). Step one proves that one is abiding by the prophetic *shariah*. In 33:21 we read, "In the Apostle of Allah there is certainly for you a good exemplar." Step two aims at increasing one's love for Allah, aiming to acquire only His pleasure and satisfaction. In 3:31 we read, "Say, 'If you love Allah, then follow me; Allah will love you.'" Although the first two steps help in dedicating one's actions sincerely for Allah's sake, the next two steps pave the way for something even greater: dedicating one's "I" for Allah's sake. Even if one succeeds in becoming a *mukhliṣ* servant of Allah, one is still affected with concealed forms of *shirk*. In order to solve this last hurdle, one must eliminate all traces of the ego; one must kill the "I." Since this goes against the essential love one possesses for oneself, killing the "I" is not something we will ever be able to do on our own. This last hurdle must therefore be executed by Allah Himself, and it is

[14] Weekly lecture given by M. T. Misbah-Yazdi at a public gathering in 2011.

[15] M. B. Majlisi, *Bihar al-Anwar* (Ocean of lights) (Beirut: Dār Ihyāʾ al-Turāth al-Arabī Publications, 1983), vol. 70:219; M. H. H. Tehrani, *Treatise of the Kernel of Kernels* (Compilation of Allamah Tabatabai's lecture notes on spiritual wayfaring) (Qum: Allamah Tabatabai Publications, 2009), p.144.

only when this is completed that one becomes annihilated in Allah. There no longer is any "I" or "me"; one becomes a manifestation of Allah's attributes. Your words are His words, your actions are His actions, and so on and so forth. All traces of "you" are eliminated. One has reached one's destination in Him.[16] At this stage whatever you read will enable you to see; the preliminary measures have been taken care of; that is, one is annihilated in Him. The following sacred tradition portray this point eloquently:

> One who seeks for Me [Allah], will find Me; and one who finds Me, will know Me; and one who knows Me, will like Me; and one who likes Me, will love Me; and one who loves Me, I shall love them; and whoever I love, I shall kill; and whoever I kill, upon Me will be their blood money; and whoever's blood money is upon Me, I am the blood money.[17]

At this stage, one has become annihilated in Allah. As He states, "I am their hearing by means of which they hear; I am their eyes by means of which they see; I am their tongues by means of which they speak."[18]

The minimum that observing *murāqabah* should entail if one is to gain the maximum benefit from reciting the texts is certitude. Certitude is of three types: (1) certitude by knowledge (such as having certitude that heart transplants are a reality after *reading* about them in medical books), (2) certitude by intuition (such as having certitude that heart transplants are a reality after *seeing* the operation being done), and (3) certitude by being (such as having certitude that heart transplants are a reality after you

[16] Note that the use of terms such as "seeing" Allah or being "annihilated" in Allah are not accepted by theologically orientated scholars who are at issue with the concept of *wahdat al-wujud* (unity of existence—i.e., a doctrinal principle among the Gnostics, who claim that there is only one existent, Allah, and all else is a manifestation or theophany of this one, true, real existent).

[17] F. Kashani, *Qurrat al-ʿAyn*, p. 366.

[18] M. Kulayni, *Al-Kafi* (Compendium of traditions), vol. 4:53.

yourself perform the operation). The insistence on certitude as a preliminary condition for seeing the realities of the metaphysical realms of existence (such as heaven and hell) is found in chapter *al-Takāthur*, which states,

> Rivalry [and vainglory] distracted you until you visited [even] the graves. No indeed! Soon you will know! Again, no indeed! Soon will you know. No indeed! Were you to know with certain knowledge, you would surely see hell. Again, you will surely see it with the eye of certainty. (102:1-7)

So far, we have attempted to show that a heart that is purified of sin and not preoccupied with other than Allah—such states being acquired by *murāqabah*—and that has certitude in faith will be able to acquire, as the ultimate objective, presence before higher celestial realms of existence and before Allah. People with such hearts are able to "see" heaven, hell, angels, prophets, and even Allah in this world by means of reciting the Holy Qurʾan ("seeing" here is on a par with an abstract form of unveiling data pertaining to higher realms of existences). On reading the story of Moses, they can "see" what had happened in the Nile with the dividing of the river into two. (In the realm of the Intellect and higher realms, there is neither time nor place; "seeing" here is abstract and executed with the heart—it is a form of intuitional knowledge.) On reading about heaven, they can see heaven, and so on and so forth. The ascension of the Holy Prophet (*miʿraj*) involved "seeing" the different stages and levels of heaven and hell and seeing Allah. This ascension is open to all Muslims, as the tradition states, "The *salat* is the believer's ascension."[19] Ayatullah Hasanzadeh describes one of his visions as follows:

> On the third night of the month of Shaʾban 1409 A.H., I was reciting *surah al-wāqiah* in my house in Qum. When I reached

[19] M. B. Majlisi, *Bihar al-Anwar* (Ocean of lights) (Beirut: Dār Ihyāʾ al-Turāth al-Arabī Publications, 1983), vol. 79:247.

> the verse "but if he be of the impugners, the astray ones, then a treat of boiling water and entry into hell" (56:92-94), all of a sudden I realised that the apparition of Hell before myself and the temperature of its flames was rising and there I intuitionally witnessed Allah's verse "and Hell is brought into view for one who sees" (79:36) for myself, in reality, without it [i.e., Hell] either making contact with me or harming me, even though the apparition was realised deep within the perceiver's soul. After all, apparitions are a form of perception. . . . At that time, two matters were inspired upon me. Firstly, were man to purify oneself from material and spiritual contaminations and to preserve one's *murāqabah* and sincerity and to execute righteous actions, it will be possible [for one] to be the recipient of apparitions of whichever Qurʾanic verse one recites or whatever event—irrespective of whether or not the event has been realised. . . . Secondly, the apparitions that take place within the perceiver's soul are one thing whilst their manifestation with the soul is quite another. The former is not a cause of harm or distress for the perceiver; rather it leads to a joy-granting knowledge for one. The manifestation, however, is a cause of harm and chastisement.[20]

There exist numerous traditions highlighting the rewards assigned for reciting this or that Qurʾanic chapter. Although the mere reading of such Arabic verses, even without understanding them, is to be rewarded, the complete and maximum reward for reciting each chapter (as assigned in the traditions) is to be bestowed upon those who can "see" those verses and be in His presence during the recitation. By way of example, it is narrated that "one should not be surprised if the dead are brought back to life on reciting surah *al-fatihah* over their bodies."[21] Naturally, this cannot be referring to merely uttering or articulating a set of sentences. There is something much deeper to such traditions

[20] H. Hasanzadeh, *Insān dar Urfe Irfān* (Man: According to the tradition of Gnosticism) (Tehran: Soroush Press, 2009), p. 23.

[21] A. A. Huwazi, Nur al-Thaqalayn (Commentary of the Holy Qurʾan) (Qum: Navide Islam Publications, 2010), vol. 1:28.

than meets the eye. The practice of *lectio divina* or Qurʾan recitation ultimately aims as making us as much like Allah as possible, that is, to be His representative on earth by drawing close to Him and becoming manifestations of His attributes.

Chapter 3

Prayer

A Monastic Perspective on Prayer

Lucy Brydon, OSB

In Christian prayer, whether in public or alone, the individual prays in union with Christ. Being a Christian means being a member of a universal, invisible, real union of all the baptized in Christ. Being a monk or a nun means devoting one's entire life as a Christian to "truly seek God," as Saint Benedict puts it in his Rule for Monasteries (RB 58.7), and to "prefer nothing whatever to Christ" (RB 72.11) Our common life is designed to help us do this at every moment. Each of our fellow monastics, and in particular the abbot, is "another Christ." Saint Benedict speaks strongly about nothing being more important than three things: the love of God (RB 72.11), the work of God (common prayer; RB 43.3), and the care of the sick (RB 36.1-2). In each case it is about finding Christ in each other and loving each other in Christ. Being "in Christ" permeates our whole life of prayer. So everything I say about Christian prayer applies equally to the Benedictine monk or nun.

Speaking of the close union between himself and his followers, Jesus uses the image of a vine and links it with the idea of prayer in union with himself: "I am the true vine, and my Father is the vinegrower. . . . Abide in me as I abide in you. Just as the branch cannot bear fruit by itself unless it abides in the vine, neither can you unless you abide in me. . . . Apart from me you can do nothing" (John 15:1, 4-5).

Saint Paul uses another vivid metaphor: the human body. Later theology spoke of "the *mystical* body," but Saint Paul does not use that qualifying word. In his first letter to the Corinthians and elsewhere, he speaks powerfully about the union of Christians and how much we need each other: "Just as the body is one and has many members, and all the members of the body, though many, are one body, so it is with Christ" (1 Cor 12:12). "[Christ] is the head of the body, the church; he is the beginning, the firstborn from the dead" (Col 1:18).

Saint Paul develops the image in a practical, graphic way. Each part of the body has its own importance, and if one part suffers, the whole body suffers (see 1 Cor 12:26). No part can say to another: "I have no need of you" (1 Cor 12:21).

Solitary prayer, then, is not "private" in the sense of being individualistic. It would be better to speak of "personal prayer." Each of us prays as a distinct person who is at the same time "one in Christ" with all Christians. This has the further, wider implication that whenever we pray in Christ, we are *ipso facto* "in God," embraced in that threefold love-relationship in the One Godhead that Christians call the Trinity. Whether we are alone, praying silently in a group, or in a private place, Christian prayer is always in the whole Christ and in the Spirit of God, addressed to the One whom Jesus called "Abba." In public prayers we make this explicit by praying *to* the Father, *through* Christ, and *in* the Spirit of God. Saint Paul speaks movingly in his letter to the Romans about this relationship with the Spirit of God in Christian prayer. We do not pray in our own strength, but "the Spirit helps us in our weakness; for we do not know how to pray as we ought, but that very Spirit [that is within us] intercedes with sighs too deep for words. And God, who searches the heart, knows what is the mind of the Spirit" (Rom 8:26-27).

The result of this union is that even when we pray in private, our prayer encompasses all the world, for the Spirit directs our prayer to God, who is "the Father of all mankind because he made us all, and loves and preserves us all."[1]

Having said all this, it has become clear to me that not every prayerful Christian is actually *aware* that this is what is happening when we pray. It may be something like the process of breathing. We all breathe and would die physically if we did not. But we do not know the physiology of breathing in detail, nor do we need to. It is deeply significant that the word "breath" in the sacred texts of Jews and Christians—רוח (*ruah*) and πνεύμα (*pneuma*)—can also mean "wind" or "spirit" and can refer to the Holy Spirit of God. When speaking of the work of God's Spirit, Jesus used this very image: "The wind blows where it chooses" (John 3:8).

Jesus, Our Life and Our Model

When we speak of Jesus and his influence on us, we do not speak of a totally separate individual who lived and died centuries ago and whose life has a kind of objective, detached value for us. We mean the risen Christ who, with his Father and the promised Holy Spirit, dwells within us: "I will ask the Father, and he will give you another Advocate, to be with you for ever. . . . Those who love me will keep my word, and my Father will love them, and we will come to them and make our home with them" (John 14:16, 23).

[1] From the "Penny Catechism," so called because the original booklet cost one penny. It is a compendium of Catholic teaching in the question-and-answer format popular at the time, and it formed the basis of Catholic education in schools for people of my generation (I started school in 1944). The method of teaching consisted of learning by heart and being examined on questions and answers. Explanations were given. Children had to learn the whole catechism by about the age of seven. A 2004 printing of the *Penny Catechism* (Houston, TX: Magnificat Institute Press) is available online at http://www.magnificatpress.com/pdf/Penny.pdf. The quoted passage is from page 21 of this printing.

In his earthly life Jesus was inspired by and quoted earlier prophets. His own example is vitally important for Christians. Before his crucifixion, he prayed for himself, especially in the garden of Gethsemane, and also for his friends and his enemies. Only God knows what the personal prayer of Jesus was on those occasions when he withdrew from the public or rose before dawn to pray. We are told he sometimes prayed all night. He prayed before major decisions such as choosing his disciples, before and while healing people, and in times of personal distress. He prayed during his baptism and when he became transfigured on Mount Tabor. Jesus also applied to himself and made use of prayers from the Scriptures. While hanging on the cross, he prayed the first verse of Psalm 22 aloud: "My God, my God, why have you forsaken me?" No doubt the rest was in his mind and heart.

Some of Jesus' prayers were petitions, as in Gethsemane: "Abba, Father, for you all things are possible; remove this cup from me; yet, not what I want, but what you want" (Mark 14:36). One of his last words on the cross was "Father, forgive them; for they do not know what they are doing" (Luke 23:34). He told us clearly, "Ask, and it will be given you; search, and you will find; knock, and the door will be opened for you" (Matt 7:7). His comment "Your Father knows what you need before you ask him" (Matt 6:8) makes us aware that asking is not really necessary from God's point of view, but it is helpful—to us! Jesus valued simplicity in prayer and recommended, "When you are praying, do not heap up empty phrases as the Gentiles do: for they think that they will be heard because of their many words" (Matt 6:7).

Observing Jesus at prayer must have deeply moved his disciples. On one occasion, after Jesus finished praying privately, they asked, "Lord, teach us to pray as John taught his disciples" (Luke 11:1). He then taught them (and us) the Our Father, the model of all Christian prayer, which begins with praise and adoration and then asks for the spiritual and material needs of the whole world—forgiveness, protection, and "daily bread." When I was a child, it was pointed out to me that Jesus did not ask for jam or cake! He taught us to pray for all that is *necessary* for our spiritual and physical well-being. Furthermore, it is no accident that the entire prayer is in the plural. As I again learned from the "Penny Catechism," since we are all brothers and sisters, "we are to pray not for ourselves only, but also for all others."[2]

In his parables too, we see Jesus' attitude to and teaching on prayer. The parables of the friend at midnight and the unjust judge (Luke 11:5-13; 18:1-8) emphasize the need for perseverance; that of the Pharisee and the publican (Luke 18:9-14) shows that prayer without humility is a hollow sham; that of the prodigal son (Luke 15:11-32) shows the need to forgive and to be forgiven. The younger son first admits his sin, then repents of it, and then has the courage to return home to pray for forgiveness from his father, who forgives him even before he finishes the prayer he had formulated. The law-abiding older son does not forgive and therefore remains a stranger to the joy that comes with forgiving and being forgiven.

Jesus also told us, "Whenever you pray, go into your room and shut the door and pray to your Father who is in secret" (Matt 6:6). Some think the "room" Jesus speaks of is what the early saints called "the cave of the heart." Others take it literally as referring to a quiet, withdrawn place. It can be both. Scattered throughout the New Testament are many other short injunctions about personal prayer from both Jesus and Paul. For instance: "Get up and pray that you may not come into temptation" (Luke 22:46); "Pray without ceasing" (2 Thess 5:17); "Whether you eat or drink, or whatever you do, do everything for the glory of God" (1 Cor 10:31); "Do not worry about anything, but in everything by prayer and supplication with thanksgiving let your requests be made known to God" (Phil 4:6).

Personal Prayer

How we learn to put all this into practice as Christians will depend a great deal on our religious and social background.

[2] Ibid.

When I reached monastic life, I already had long-standing habits of personal prayer.

Looking back at my childhood, I realize that although we were economically quite poor, my family was very rich spiritually. Catholic devotional practice was and is very varied, so my first steps in personal prayer began as devotional practice rather than theory. Christ was at the center of life as our brother, friend, and Lord. As a small child, I talked to Jesus a lot. In a good Catholic home, the spiritual world was very real and inextricably connected with the "ordinary" world. The saints were our older brothers and sisters who would help us. The example of my parents' faith practice drew me deeply into the way of prayer. I will confine myself to what has remained with me until this day.

Sign of the Cross

Almost my first memory is of my mother taking my right hand and showing me how to trace the sign of the cross on my body. I understood that this sign was to remind us of Jesus' dying for us and that we made the sign as a prayer to ask God for his protection and blessing before and after all activities: meals, prayers, the beginning and end of the day, important tasks, times of joy and sorrow. It was both private and public. When later I entered an apostolic religious congregation and then Benedictine monastic life, I found this teaching embodied in the Liturgy of the Hours. Each Hour of the church's prayer begins with the sign of the cross and the prayer "O God, come to our aid." This was a world I already knew very well.

Times, Seasons, and Postures

As children, we learned Morning and Night Prayer first at our mother's knees and later by our bedside. We usually prayed kneeling, but from my parents' example of private times of prayer, I saw that it was also acceptable to pray while seated. We stood to ask a blessing before sitting down to meals and afterward remained seated as we said, "Thank you, God." In public worship at church, we knelt, sat and, stood to pray: it all hung together. The church's year (following the life of Christ) was part of our own life, and we prayed according to the seasons. Using the beads of the rosary[3] was one of the ways we did this regularly.

Morning Offering

The admonition to pray "without ceasing" was a puzzle. But in childhood I learned a personal prayer custom that made this possible. It was the "morning offering," and it meant that on waking, we offered to God "every thought, word, action, and suffering of this day" in union with Christ for the salvation of the world and for the "holy souls" (the dead). Once this was done, everything except sin became prayer. My mother's explanation about how this "worked" continues to inspire me. To my childish objection that Jesus was "then" and I am "now," she simply said, "There's no time with God."

Spiritual Renewal

In the 1960s and 70s, a renewal movement in the Catholic Church led to a tremendous change in every aspect of our reli-

[3] The rosary is a Catholic devotion commemorating (1) the birth and childhood of Jesus—Joyful Mysteries; (2) the public ministry of Jesus—Luminous Mysteries; (3) the passion and death of Jesus—Sorrowful Mysteries; and (4) the risen life of Jesus and the heavenly life—Glorious Mysteries. It is prayed using rosary beads. The rosary chaplet consists of five groups of beads, each group consisting of one separate bead followed by ten others. With each group of eleven beads, one prays one Our Father, ten Hail Marys, and one Glory Be to the Father.

gious lives. Approaches to personal prayer became more varied, and the Word of God (as we learned to call the Bible) became absolutely central to public and private prayer. Our Protestant brothers and sisters must have wondered what took us so long. About the same time, a great resurgence of devotion to the Spirit of God—the charismatic or Pentecostal renewal—was sweeping through the church. It emphasized hearing God speaking to us personally through the Bible, and it promoted an ecstatic form of praising God that included praying in "tongues."[4] It was all very inspiring and exciting.

These years also saw the rise of psychological studies linking personality theory and personal spiritual development. The realization that different people come into relationship with God in different ways led to a rediscovery and diffusion of ancient Christian traditions of prayer that had been neglected or limited to certain areas of the church. There was great freedom to explore different ways of using the Scriptures in personal prayer that had been developed by the Benedictine, Ignatian, Franciscan, and Dominican traditions. It was like being invited to a rich spiritual banquet: wise discernment was needed to avoid indigestion. When I learned about *lectio divina* in this period, before becoming a Benedictine, somehow all my earlier experiences of personal prayer coalesced—reading, reflecting, talking to God, being "present" and silent. Another exciting development at this time was the opening of the heart to people of other religions and their ways of prayer (whether they called it "prayer" or not).[5]

[4] Praying or singing in tongues is a vocalized but wordless form of praise of God. Saint Augustine in his sermon on Psalm 32 speaks of something similar happening in his own time and calls it the "prayer of jubilation" (with sounds and music, but no words).

[5] The decree *Nostra Aetate* of the Second Vatican Council encouraged Catholics to engage in interreligious dialogue and acknowledged the truth of God found in other religions.

Benedictine Monastic Experience

Coming into the Benedictine life in the late 1980s, therefore, I entered a prayer world already known to me. Having discovered a way of wordless prayer, I was excited to find that this contemplative silence was an ancient practice of the Desert Fathers and medieval mystics. In early monastic teachings on prayer[6] and in the Rule of Saint Benedict, I sensed that in some way I was going back to my beginnings. There was the same emphasis on the importance of the Lord's Prayer as model, as well as the same appeal to the teaching of Jesus about the qualities of humility, true love, and sorrow ("compunction" in monastic texts); confidence in God; and the need for prayer to be allied with practical virtue. The language may have been somewhat unfamiliar, but the teaching was the same. The Rule of Saint Benedict is studded throughout with literally hundreds of biblical words of guidance on monastic prayer.[7] The much-quoted words "Nothing is to be preferred to the Work of God" (RB 43.3) are generally taken to refer to public prayer. Saint Benedict called the monastic work of singing the psalms and listening together to the Scriptures the "work of God." It can mean our work for God. But it also means God's work of transforming us, and it includes personal prayer, where "all of us, with unveiled faces, seeing the glory of the Lord as though reflected in a mirror, are being transformed into the same image from one degree of glory to another; for this comes from the Lord, the Spirit" (2 Cor 3:18).

As the monastic work of praying the psalms publicly five or seven times daily permeates our life and prayer, images from the psalms seem to rise unbidden into the mind and heart as expressions of a personal relationship with God: my rock, my love, my fortress, my stronghold, my Savior, my shield, my place of refuge, my heritage forever. God corrects us, too, with phrases

[6] E.g., the *Treatise on the Lord's Prayer* by Saint Cyprian, a North African bishop and martyr who died in 258, and the *Ninth Conference on Prayer* by Saint John Cassian (360–423).

[7] See the thematic index in *RB 1980*, pp. 578–79.

from the psalms and other scriptural texts. "Indeed, the Word of God is living and active, sharper than any two-edged sword" (Heb 4:12).

Influence of Interreligious Dialogue

In recent years, developing deeper relationships with people of other faiths has had a profound effect on my personal prayer. Sharing "resonances" has been a thrilling affirmation of our unity in the One God, even in cases where people may not actually say "God" at all. For example, my experience with Buddhists has drawn me deeper into the mystery of silent, contemplative prayer and has enlarged my understanding of the inward journey of the soul. I have become aware that what Buddhists call "the Unborn, the Undying, the Unconditioned, the Uncreated" is the mystery that for me, a Christian, is "God." When I discovered that Muslims, Hindus, Buddhists, and Jains all make use of beads in personal prayer, as Catholics do, it was another point of convergence. An experience of being present at a *dhikr* with a group of Muslim men and women chanting the Names of God had a powerful effect on me. As Muslims and Christians, we offer praise and adoration to God—and not only in public. I found the devotion of reciting the Beautiful Names of God to be somewhat similar to the "litanies"[8] of my early childhood. Now I can incorporate some of these practices into my personal prayer. As one of the sisters in my community put it, "We can all come with Elijah to the mouth of the cave and stand with Moses in prayer before the burning bush."

Finally, some words of a Christian poet that I think describe my experience of personal prayer very beautifully:

[8] Litanies are lists of titles of Jesus and also of Mary and other saints. Each title carries a response: in the case of Jesus, "Have mercy on us"; in the case of Mary and other saints, "Pray for us." These devotions can be used publicly or privately.

What we call the beginning is often the end
And to make an end is to make a beginning.
The end is where we start from. . . .

With the drawing of this Love and the voice of this Calling

We shall not cease from exploration
And the end of all our exploring
Will be to arrive where we started
And know the place for the first time.[9]

[9] T. S. Eliot, *Four Quartets*, "Little Gidding" (New York: Harcourt, Brace and Co., 1943), pp. 58–59.

A Shiʿite Perspective on Prayer[1]

Fatemeh Nazari

One of the most enduring manifestations of the human soul and one of the most fundamental aspects of human existence is the longing to supplicate and to worship. History shows us that human beings have always prayed and worshiped. Any differences in worship lie in the method used and the deity invoked.

In terms of the method of worship, there have been various approaches and forms, ranging from dancing rituals and rhythmical group movements, together with verbal expressions of admiration and reverence, to the most humble submissions to the deity. In terms of deities worshiped, there have been several, both material and immaterial. Idols of stone and wood have been worshiped throughout time, as has the eternal All-Sustainer, who is not bound or limited by time and space.

Worship was not invented by the prophets. Rather, they taught the best form of worship. They clarified its finest method, which includes the actions to be carried out and the manner in which they should be done. In addition, they opposed the worship of deities (*shirk*, polytheism) other than the One God. Indeed, Prophet Adam was a monotheist, showing that humans were originally monotheistic; only later did they deviate to the worship of idols.

[1] This paper was prepared by one of the participants but was not presented during the conference. It is included here to provide a fuller picture of the Shiʿa understanding of prayer.

Supplication, a form of worship, can be defined as a spiritual condition that creates a bond of attraction and intimacy between a person and his or her deity. It is one of the most sublime and noble of spiritual actions that can bring a person closer to God. True supplication is recognizing God and being humble toward Him, while simultaneously realizing one's insignificance. For such sincere supplication to occur, there are three stages and prerequisites.

The first stage is to have true belief and faith in God. The reason for this is quite obvious: if one does not believe in God, communication with Him and attempts to attain nearness to Him are futile and meaningless. It is important to note here that while believing in God is necessary, this belief can have many different levels and qualities.

The second stage is that the individual should believe that he, a needy person, has the ability to communicate with an immaculate being that is absolute, needless, and entirely self-sufficient. This ability can be better understood if we take into account the fact that the soul does not belong to the material world: it is essentially immaterial. Thus, it is possible for the soul to communicate and build a relationship with God.

The third prerequisite is invoking God and having hope in Him. This happens in its true form when a person ceases to trust or hope in anything except God. The individuals and beings involved in this person's life become irrelevant, and God begins to be seen as the sole and absolute cause of everything. In fact, a person sees that all circumstances and situations occur because of Him and as a part of His plan. It is in this state of mind that supplication is realized in its full potential. Even if a person's tongue is not engaged in physical prayer, the heart continues to be occupied with worship and supplication to God. To clarify, I will expand on the concept of *duʿā*, Arabic for "supplication," which has been described as the gem and spirit of all worship. Furthermore, from the viewpoint of verses from the Qurʾan and narrations, I will discuss (a) the quality of a true *duʿā*, (b) the etiquette and conditions of a *duʿā* required for a response from God (*istijābah*), (c) the obstacles to *istijābah*, (d) the effects of *duʿā*,

(e) the qualities and importance of *duʿā*, and finally, (f) its spiritual effects.

The Importance of Prayer

In order to attain spiritual peace, acquire moral virtues, improve our willpower and intellectual capabilities, and above all, achieve nearness to God, it is necessary to pray to Him. Prayer is also needed to refrain from sins and to rid ourselves of moral defects and satanic temptations. Additionally, it is essential to ask for material and spiritual support from God.

During prayer, we call on God and speak to Him in a manner and wording of our choice in order to gradually receive and realize His response. Since God's response is often subtle, we need to be attentive to the hints that are given. There are many forms of communication beyond the conventional use of language, and these are discovered solely through empathy and intimacy. When addressing people, God begins by speaking to a person's consciousness. Imam Ali has said, "In various eras, God has spoken to His servants in the depths of their conscience, and following this consistent conversation, the light of awareness emerges in their eyes, ears, and hearts."[2] But *duʿā* is not simply calling upon God; it is also an opportunity to *know* Him. Communication demands at least two parties, and it is in these conversations that intimacy and knowledge of God can be achieved. Through these exchanges, one's soul can be purified and one's faith can be strengthened. Furthermore, one's heart and intellect will find peace and serenity. It is for this reason that when people approach God, they should forget everything else.

When God becomes more than the First Cause (of the creation of the world) and an intimate conversation ensues with Him as a friend and beloved one, a person can finally be considered a

[2] Nahj al-Balaghah, *Wise-Sayings* 222, Subhi Saleh edition (Qum: Dar al-Hijrah).

true supplicant. It is in this moment that one is able to truly benefit from and enjoy serving God, choosing the best and most pure way to live in this world.

A *duʿā* in its essence speaks of a lover's needs and hopes. It speaks of love, fear, and knowledge (*maʿrifah*). It speaks of repentance and regret, benevolence, and a response (*ijābah*). It speaks of both worldly necessities and noble, heavenly ideals. It speaks of submission (*taslim*) and learning. In fact, it could be said that nothing other than *duʿā* contains such a vast amount of divine blessings with so much relief and countless merciful advantages.

Communication with God is so valuable and advantageous that it is even attractive for those who desire the temporary and perishable necessities of this world. Perhaps such necessities become a tool to call upon God and can thus be a means for return to God. In fact, they may elevate a person from inferior spiritual levels to superior ones, even if this intention does not initially exist. Thus, it is not problematic to begin *duʿā* with these requests in mind; however, it is problematic if one remains in this condition for an extended period of time. *Duʿā* may initially be a path with a certain purpose or goal in mind, and someone may seek *duʿā* simply desiring something else. However, fortunate is the person for whom *duʿā* itself becomes the goal, as opposed to the means. Invoking God and speaking with Him becomes one's deepest wish, as other desires fade away. A real *duʿā* is a *duʿā* in which the world is deemed insignificant. This is the mystical side of supplication that gives life a concrete meaning and a worthy purpose. Without a concrete purpose, a person can only live aimlessly.

The Meaning of *Duʿā*

Duʿā (an Arabic verb in the past tense verb and in the third-person masculine singular) means "he attracted someone," "he asked for help," or "he called (someone) toward himself." *Duʿā-hu* means "he called him to eat." *Duʿā lahu* means "to pray for someone," and *Duʿā ʿalayhi* means "to pray against someone."[3]

In *Minhāj al-Sādiqin* we read that the meaning of *duʿā* is to become detached from everything except God and to move only toward Him. Shedding tears and asking for help is the most sublime form of worship. Indeed, according to a hadith, "*Duʿā* is worship."[4]

To summarize, *duʿā*, in a religious context, is the calling out of a servant to his God. It is communication between the servant of God and God Himself, both through one's heart and one's tongue, and it is the most basic part of true servitude.

In his commentary on the Qurʾan, *Al-Mizan fi Tafsir al-Qurʾan*, ʿAllamah Tabatabaʾi states:

> *Duʿā* is turning oneself to the Deity and calling upon God with honesty and sincerity. This occurs when the hopes of a supplicant are alienated from all other apparent causes and tools. It is when the supplicant realizes and truly believes that nobody other than God is able to solve his problems. Consequently, his hands, heart, and tongue turn together to God, and it is in this state that his *duʿā* is sincere and unlikely not to be answered.

God has set absolutely no conditions or prerequisites for *duʿā*. All that is required is that one must "call Me in *duʿā*," as mentioned in this verse of the Holy Qurʾan:[5]

> When my servants ask you about Me, [tell them that] I am indeed nearmost. I answer the supplicant's call when he calls Me. (2:186)

In the book *Kashf al-Asrār*, it is mentioned that *duʿā* is of two types. One contains the praise of God:

[3] *Majmaʿ al-Bahrayn*, pp. 138–41.

[4] *Minhāj al-Sādiqin*, vol. 1, p. 425.

[5] *Tarjume-ye Tafsir al-Mizan*, vol. 15, p. 595.

> Oh the Living, oh the Self-subsistent, oh the Possessor of glory and generosity, oh my Lord, oh Allah, oh our Lord. All praise is due to You. There is no god but You.

The other type of *duʿā* is one that requests something from God: "Oh my Lord, grant me so and so."

The word *duʿā* and its derivatives have been used approximately 212 times in the Holy Qurʾan.[6]

The Etiquette of *Duʿā*

It is highly recommended that every supplicant adhere to certain norms of etiquette. In what follows, we will refer to some of them.

A. Knowledge (Maʿrifah)

The following verse from the Holy Qurʾan was recited in the presence of Imam al-Sadiq:

> Is He who answers the call of the distressed [person] when he invokes Him and removes his distress? (27:62)

Someone then asked the Imam, "Why is it that God does not respond to our *duʿā*?" The Imam replied by saying, "Your *duʿā* is not responded to because you do not know the God that you call in your *duʿā*."[7]

The feeling of yearning and dependence of a servant toward his Lord is actually fundamental to our faith. Supplicating extensively without any real knowledge of God is a sign of weakness. Someone who does not realize with certainty that his heart and his consciousness are subservient to His power is actually ordering God with his *duʿā*. Although a person may believe that

[6] *Kashf al-Asrār wa ʿUddat al-Abrār*, vol. 1, p. 498.

[7] *Falāh al-Sāʾil*, p. 107.

it is simply a supplication, this kind of *duʿā* in its real essence is ordering and commanding God and shows one's insolence and arrogance toward Him.[8] God says in the Holy Qurʾan, "So supplicate God, putting exclusive faith in Him" (40:14).

B. Internal and External Purity (Tahārah)

A very important condition for the effectiveness of worship (like *dhikr* and *duʿā*) is to have internal purity in addition to external purity. Merely moving one's tongue is not useful, or effective, and may even cause the hardness of one's heart. God says, "Indeed Allah loves the penitent and He loves those who keep clean" (2:222). Certainly, God will respond to the *duʿā* of someone whom He is fond of.

One's property and wealth must also be purified. Imam al-Sadiq has said, "Whoever wishes for his *duʿā* to be accepted should purify his earnings and eat *halal* food."[9] Imam al-Rida has said:

> Do not be tired of praying to God [*duʿā*] as it has a high position in the eyes of God. Be patient, earn a *halal* living, establish bonds of kinship [*silah Rahim*] and do not quarrel with people. Indeed we, the progeny of Prophet Muhammad, keep bonds of kinship with anyone who breaks contact with us, and we do good to those who do evil to us. By God, I see a good future in this.[10]

The Prophet has said, "Whoever wants his *duʿā* to be accepted should purify his food and his income."[11] A divine narration (*hadith qudsi*) says:

[8] *Al-Sāfi fi Tafsir al-Qurʾan*, vol. 1, p. 204.

[9] *Wasāʾil al-Shiʿah*, vol. 4, p. 1129.

[10] Ibid.

[11] *Che Bāyad Kard: Tarjome va Tanzimi Vizhe az Al-Murāqibāt*, vol. 2, p. 150.

> When you supplicate me and make requests, I will respond and answer. No supplication will be hidden from Me except the supplication of someone who eats *haram* food.[12]

The Requirement of Prayer

In order to examine the qualities by which one should supplicate God, we will look at verses from the Holy Qurʾan. It is narrated that the companions of the Prophet asked him, "How should we pray to God? Is God near us so that we should whisper to him? Or is He far from us so that we should call Him loudly?" The following verse was subsequently revealed:

> When My servants ask you about Me, [tell them that] I am indeed nearmost. I answer the supplicant's call when he calls Me. So let them respond to Me, and let them have faith in Me, so that they may fare rightly. (2:186)

This verse explains the concept of *duʿā* in its most pleasant manner, its most delicate structure, and its most beautiful form. There are some subtle points in this verse that denote the importance of the matter.

a. The words of God are in the first-person narrator form, not the third person. This indicates that a great amount of attention is paid to the subject.

b. Instead of saying something like "When people ask you . . .," the word *ebadi* has been used. It means "When *My servants* ask you . . ." This shows the greatness of His kindness and that, again, attention is given to the subject.

c. The expected response for "When My servants ask you about Me . . ." would be "Tell them that He is indeed nearmost." However, in this verse the intermediary (i.e.,

[12] *Wasāʾil al-Shiʿah*, vol. 7, p. 145.

"tell them") has been removed, and the verse says, "*I* am indeed nearmost."

d. The sentence has been emphasized with the word meaning "indeed."

e. In the original Arabic, God's state of proximity is mentioned with a modifier and not with a verb. Thus, the more permanent quality of the relationship is emphasized.

f. The action of answering is mentioned in the present tense, which indicates the repetition and continuity of God's response.

g. The response of *duʿā* is mentioned with the condition "when he calls Me." This condition is not truly an additional condition, as the action of supplicating God requires that someone is doing this. What this implies is that a response is not limited by any condition, and the *duʿā* of a supplicant will be answered unconditionally, as is mentioned in 40:60: "Call Me, and I will hear you." This verse indicates that "supplicating" is the only condition for receiving a response.

Each of these points in its own right indicates that intimate care and attention have been paid to the issue of *duʿā*. Another characteristic of this verse is that the first-person pronoun is used seven times—the only verse in the Holy Qurʾan for which this occurs.

In addition to mentioning the issue of a *duʿā*'s response, the verse also mentions the reasons for it. For instance, the reason that God is near is because they are His servants; therefore, they are completely dependent on Him. Moreover, because He is so close to them, He answers their *duʿā*s. Since there is no condition for a *duʿā* to be answered, God will answer the supplication of anyone who supplicates. The only condition for His response is that the supplicant should call to God. Although this condition is not an addendum, it indicates that a supplicant should be sincere in his supplication and should only desire it from God. A true prayer entails the presence of one's heart and soul and not merely the presence of one's tongue.

The Outcomes of *Duʿā*

A. Nearness to God

Islamic philosophy holds that existence has several levels. The lowest level of existence is the material, physical world. At the other end of the spectrum, at the highest level of existence, is the Divine Existence. As a person advances to the higher levels of existence while acquiring virtues, he or she also becomes closer to God at the same rate and enjoys infinite benefits.

Through performing the recommended prayers, one is able to reach a position of closeness to God. This fact has also been mentioned in the following divine narration (*hadith qudsi*): "My faithful servant is always becoming nearer to me."[13] And, "Indeed, he [a faithful servant] becomes near to Me through the recommended prayers (*nawafil*)."[14]

In another authentic divine narration, God says:

> Of the actions that bring my servants closer to me, there is nothing dearer to me than the completion of the obligations that I have assigned to him. And indeed I love him, I become the ear with which he hears, the eye with which he sees, the tongue with which he speaks, and the hand with which he holds. If he calls upon Me, I answer him, and if he asks from Me, I grant his request.[15]

B. The Brightness and Insightfulness of the Heart

When one turns toward God, a light from within shines onto one's soul and illuminates one's heart. Thus, in Islamic teachings, both the remembrance of God and supplication are described as "the light of the heart" and "the refinement of the heart." This spiritual light liberates the heart from every darkness and impurity that has resulted from paying attention to things other than God.

[13] *Akhlāq-e Islami*, p. 55.

[14] *Al-Kāfi*, Kitab al-Imān wa al-Kufr, vol. 4 , p. 41.

[15] Risāle-ye Liqā Allah, p. 30.

Thus, remembrance and supplication can cause many great spiritual effects:

a. *Revival of the heart.* In Islam, it is believed that biological life is not the only life available to us. Rather, higher life requires a second birth, which is only possible through knowing God and turning to Him, as is said in the holy Qurʾan:

> O you who have faith! Answer God and the Apostle when he summons you to that which will give you life. (8:24)

Thus, the condition for attaining the real life, or "the goodly life," is to pay attention to God. Similarly, the death of one's heart is a result of neglecting Him. The Holy Prophet says, "Through the remembrance of God, hearts are given life, and their death lies in neglecting Him."[16]

When the heart neglects God, it becomes distressed, and consequently one becomes afflicted with various mental diseases. The only cure for this grueling spiritual disease that has brought humanity to its knees is to become acquainted with God and to direct one's heart toward Him.

b. *Unique energy and freshness of the heart.* This solves the problem of inaction and/or lack of motivation that one may feel in different ways throughout life. By obtaining this spiritual freshness and happiness, one also becomes more spiritual. Imam Ali has said, "Persistence in remembering God revives and enlightens one's heart."[17]

c. *Insightfulness.* Remembrance of God brightens the heart and the mind with the light of insight. It is because of this insight that pious people are saved from Satan's temptations and assaults. Regarding this, the Holy Qurʾan says, "When those who are Godwary are touched by a visitation of Satan, they remember [Allah] and, behold, they perceive" (7:201).

[16] Tunbih al-khavat, p. 360.

[17] *Ghurar al-Hikam*, p. 186, hadith no. 3656.

The Acceptance of Prayer

A. The Conditions of Acceptance

Presence of the heart. One of the most crucial conditions in supplication is the presence of one's heart. To merely move one's tongue is futile and may possibly lead to hardness of heart, as one's words lack thought. An absent heart is similar to a lamp without light: it is pointless. Without this light, a person will be unable to understand the true realities of existence. A person who utters *dhikr* without the presence of his or her heart is similar to a blind man who carries a torch in his hand, unable to benefit from its light. Hence, one should focus on God while in supplication. In fact, if one's heart is occupied with that which is other than God during supplication, it would be considered an act of rudeness toward Him. Such a supplication would not bring about nearness to God; instead, it would take a person further away from Him.[18]

Being completely detached from everything other than God. One of the ways in which supplications may be answered is to completely detach oneself from everything other than God. More importantly, it is to put a special trust in the Lord of the universe and to pay special attention to Him. The Cause of all causes (*ʿillat al-ʿilal*) is God. All other causes and actors serve as channels of His grace so that we may change our lives. These are all divine agents that execute His orders and divine will. The only true actor in this universe is Almighty God. Imam al-Sadiq quoted the words of God spoken to the Prophet: "If a person requests something from Me while truly realizing that all benefits and losses lie in My hands, I will grant them their request."[19]

Being certain that one's duʿā *will be answered.* The Holy Prophet has said, "Call upon God while being certain that your call will be answered."[20]

[18] Risāle-ye Nūr-e ʿalā Nūr dar Dhike wa Dhākir wa Madhkūr, pp. 62 and 79.

[19] *Al-Kāfi*, vol. 2, p. 273.

[20] *Bihār al-Anwār*, vol. 93, p. 305.

To explain this hadith, ʿAllamah Tabatabaʾi says:

> The truth behind this fact is that supplicating with doubt and hopelessness indicates that one does not know what one seriously wants. Hence, it has been discouraged for a person to ask for something that is seemingly impossible.[21]

Imam Ali says, "One who has been granted [the blessing of] supplication will not be deprived of its answer."[22]

B. The Obstacles of Acceptance

Sin. According to many narrations, one of the most dangerous factors that can prevent acceptance of our prayers is committing sins. Further, it can cut off our relationship with God at the root and prevent us from paying attention to Him. Imam Ali says, "Committing sins prevents the acceptance of prayer."[23] Imam Sajjad says, "One of the sins that causes *duʿā* to be rejected, and also darkens the air, is to disobey and hurt one's parents."[24] Imam Sajjad also says, "The sins that cause one's *duʿā* to be rejected are: bad temper, hypocrisy [*nifāq*] with brothers in faith, disbelieving in *istijābah*, supplicating whilst delaying one's obligatory prayers [*salāt*] until their due time passes, and being rude and obscene in one's speech."[25]

Although all sins have negative effects on the acceptance of one's prayers, there are some sins that have been specifically mentioned as an impediment to acceptance of prayer, such as a *harām* earning, committing any injustice (*ẓulm*), and abandoning the action of enjoining the good and forbidding the evil.

Supplication without action. If God has given someone the keys to fulfill a goal, and this person, being ungrateful, refuses to use

[21] *Al-Mizan*, vol. 2, p. 47.

[22] *Wasāʾil al-Shiʿah, Kitāb al-Salāh, Abwāab al-Duʿā, Bāb* 2, no. 3.

[23] For example, see Duʿā of Kumayl in *Mafātih al-Jinān*.

[24] *Maʿāni al-Akhbār*, p. 270.

[25] *Maʿāni al-Akhbār*, p. 271.

these keys, then such a *duʿā* cannot be answered. This person wants God to open the door for him—a door to which he has been given the key. This type of supplication is against the laws of nature. The purpose of *duʿā* is to acquire an ability or competence in one's troubling situation. In the case where God has already given this capability to someone, asking for it would be asking for something that has already been given.

C. Factors That Increase the Likeliness of Acceptance

Time. The time in which one supplicates has an important role in the success of a *duʿā*, as does the emotional state of a supplicant. Nighttime specifically has an exceptional status for personal supplication, invocation, and thought. The night has a mysterious character and draws one to contemplate the inner self and the mysteries of one's soul. The Almighty has said, "Indeed the watch of the night is firmer in tread and more upright in respect to speech. For indeed during the day you have drawn-out engagements" (73:6-7).

In many ways, rising in the night for *duʿā* increases the unity between one's heart and tongue, and what is said is firmer and more focused. This is because there are many obligations and responsibilities during the day. Finding extra time during the day is difficult with the constant engagements of life and sustenance. Except for those who can always remember God and for "whom neither trading nor bargaining distracts from the remembrance of God" (24:37), the night has a vital role in the purity of one's soul and one's spiritual ascension.[26] "And keep vigil for a part of the night, as a supererogatory [devotion] for you. It may be that your Lord will raise you to a praiseworthy station" (17:79).

There are many Qurʾanic verses and narrations regarding the importance of praying and supplicating at night and of seeking forgiveness (*istighfar*) before dawn. Imam al-Sadiq has said:

[26] *Risāle-ye Nūr-e ʿalā Nūr dar Dhike wa Dhākir wa Madhkūr.*

> The Holy Prophet has said: "The best time to supplicate God is during the early hours of the morning before dawn [*sahar*]." He then recited this verse quoting Prophet Jacob when his children requested his prayers: "I shall plead with my Lord to forgive you." The Prophet then said that "Jacob delayed the prayer until the time of dawn [*sahar*]."

On the day of ʿArafah, Imam al-Sajjad saw that a beggar was asking others for money. The Imam then said to him, "Woe to you! Are you requesting from someone other than God on a day in which there is even hope in the fetuses that lie in their mothers' wombs, that the grace of God will extend to them and that they will become prosperous?"[27]

Another crucial time for supplication is during the days and nights of the holy month of Ramadan and during the night of *Eid al-Fitr*.[28] Imam Ali narrated that he was shocked at a person who did not pray on these nights. Other key times for prayer and supplication include the night of *Eid al-Adʾha*,[29] the night of the middle of *Shaʿbān*,[30] and the first night of *Rajab*.[31] Other privileged times for supplication are the times between the daily prayers and on Fridays.

[27] *Mafātih al-Jinān*.

[28] The Muslim holiday that marks the end of the month of Ramadan. This is an occasion to celebrate the completion of one month of fasting and obedience.

[29] The Festival of Sacrifice, one of the important Islamic holidays, in which Muslims celebrate the arrival of another season of hajj and their ability to offer some sacrifice to God in a way similar to the sacrifice made by Abraham.

[30] The eighth month of the Islamic calendar, considered one of the four sacred months in Islam. In the middle of this month in the year 255 AH, the twelfth Imam was born. There are many supplications and acts of worship recommended for this day and night.

[31] The seventh month of the Islamic calendar, considered one of the four sacred months in Islam. On the 27th of this month, Prophet Muhammad was appointed by God as His messenger, and on the 13th of this month, Imam Ali was born. There are many supplications and acts of worship recommended for this month, such as staying in the Grand Mosque of the town for three days in fasting and worship. This is called *iʿtikāf*.

Place. Some of the privileged places of worship and supplication are mosques, Masjid al-Haram,[32] Masjid al-Nabi,[33] Karbala,[34] and the shrines of the Holy Imams.

The Etiquette of Serving God

One of the most excellent manifestations of *tawhid* (monotheism) is *duʿā* and supplication. However the etiquette of true servitude demands that one does not request anything from the Almighty but instead simply calls upon Him and praises Him. This being said, however, there are narrations where believers are told specifically to ask for what they want. Requesting something is different from calling upon God. Those who have achieved the position of *taslim* (submission) always call upon God without requesting anything from Him. The narrations that speak of making specific requests are for ordinary people, not for a true *muwahhid* (monotheist). Even if a *muwahhid* makes a specific request, it is because the nature of *duʿā* is related to worship. Essentially, asking for something from God is in itself a type of servitude. Other than this, a *muwahhid,* having reached a point of absolute submission, does not request anything from God.

Nevertheless, this position is for a person who is truly acquainted with the Lord and prefers being present in front of Him over anything and everything else. "Who has tasted the sweetness of Your love and then taken an objective other than You?"[35]

[32] "The Sacred Mosque" surrounding the Kaʿbah, located in Mecca and considered the holiest site in Islam.

[33] "The Mosque of the Prophet," located in Medina and known as the second holiest site in Islam.

[34] This city in Iraq is known as the location of the Battle of Karbala and is one of the holiest cities for Shiʿa Muslims; it is where Imam Husayn and seventy-two of his family members and companions who were martyred on the Day of Ashura are buried.

[35] *Mafātih al-Jinān*, Munajāt al-Muhibbin, p. 252.

Thus, the etiquette of true servitude demands that one does not desire anything other than God Himself. This is the class of worship that the true friends of God—the noble and the free-spirited—have, resulting from the high ambitions of a servant.

In any case, supplication is a requirement of servitude, as are the appropriate norms of etiquette in the presence of God. However, it is important to note that the feeling of helplessness that follows turning to God is a blessing He gives us. Such a supplication does not require *istijabah,* because the *duʿā* itself is God's response. When one calls upon God out of burning love, this *duʿā* itself is the *istijabah* and the way in which God has turned toward the individual. This is a case where an individual does not want anything specific: he simply wants to call upon God. Here, a relationship with God is what is desired, and this is precisely what true servitude is.

Thus, the most delightful feeling a person can experience is the satisfaction and sweetness of having a true relationship with God that consists of both companionship and conversation. The most beautiful scene in this world is that of servants calling upon God. The finest of drops are those teardrops that, in the depths of the night, fall to the ground from the eyes of a supplicant who fears and loves God.

In summary, having true faith in God and being aware of one's neediness while invoking and hoping in God are some of the fundamentals of sincere supplication. It is important to beseech God for a variety of reasons: to attain high morality, to improve ourselves in every aspect, and to refrain from satanic temptations that lead us to sin. A person is to know God and to possess internal and external purity when invoking Him. He or she should also call to Him with full heart and soul, while being detached from everything other than God. Refraining from sinning and being willing to do what one needs to do are also important when asking God for blessings. Then one can have a bright and insightful heart and achieve nearness to Him.

Our concluding call is "All praise belongs to God, the Lord of all the worlds."

A Shiʿite Perspective on Ritual Prayer

Mohammad Taghi Ansaripour

When discussing ritual prayer (*salāt*) in Islamic law, it is appropriate to mention the difference between ritual prayer and supplication (*duʿā*). Ritual prayer contains supplication; however, it differs from supplication. Ritual prayer has determined and defined parts and includes obligatory preparations and rules that must be followed in order for it to be valid. This is not the case, however, with supplication.

Qurʾanic and Islamic traditions, especially the Shiʿite ones, repeatedly put emphasis on supplicating God,[1] but there are no particular formalities that need to be observed. That is to say, when a Muslim supplicates God, as distinct from reciting prayers, it is not necessary to observe rules regarding time or posture (sitting or standing) or position (facing Mecca).

There is a vast heritage of supplications in Shiʿite traditions that constitutes a treasury of human conversation with God. These supplications, which go back to Prophet Muhammad and his household (Shiʿite Imams), express various aspects of human

[1] There are very many verses in the Qurʾan that advise a believer to supplicate God. The Qurʾan uses different derivatives of the following words that mean or are interrelated with "supplication": *duʿā, inābah, suʾāl, tadarruʿ, istighfār*, and *tawbah*. In Shiʿite traditions the supplication is introduced as the core and essence of worshiping God. See Kulayni, Muhammad b. Yaʾqoub, *Al-Kāfi*, vol. 2 (Tehran: Dar al-Kutub al-Islamiyyah, 1365/1986), p. 466ff.

spiritual needs and thus provide us with a profound religious anthropology. These supplications demonstrate how a limited human being can enter into a relationship with an unlimited, benevolent, generous, and caring God, how a human being can talk to Him and through this relationship gain hope, richness, wisdom, a feeling of dignity, love for other creatures, purity, and righteousness. For example, one may refer to the following supplications in Shiʿite traditions: Kumayl, Sabāh, Simāt, ʿAsharāt, Mashlūl, Mojīr, Jushan, ʿArafah, Shaʿbāniyyah, Abū Hamzah, as well as to *Al-Sahīfat al-Sajjādiyyah*, a book citing Imam Sajjad that contains more than fifty supplications. There are also "whispers" from Imam Sajjad, known as the Fifteen Whispers, including the Whisper of the Hoper, the Whisper of the Eager, the Whisper of the Repentant, the Whisper of the Complainer, the Whisper of the Awed, the Whisper of the Thanks Giver, the Whisper of the Obedient, the Whisper of the Desirous, the Whisper of the Lover, the Whisper of the Needy, and the Whisper of the Mystic.

Ritual prayer is one of the most important religious duties for a Muslim. In the Qurʾan the Prophet and the believers are repeatedly enjoined to pray. There are some forty-five verses in the Qurʾan that use the word *salāt* to enjoin saying prayer, to revere it, and to show appreciation for those who are committed to performing it steadfastly, regularly, and without ostentation. These verses are in addition to those that determine the time of ritual prayer, the preparations for ritual prayer—*wuḍū* (ablution), *ghusl* (ritual bathing), and *tayammum* (dry ablution)—the direction of the *qiblah*, and so on.

In Arabic it is generally possible to derive a verb from a noun. But the Qurʾan, whenever it refers to the performance of ritual prayer, instead of doing so, mostly uses *iqāmat al-salāt* (establishment of prayers) and its derivations and does not derive a verb from *salāt* (prayer). A famous philologist of the Qurʾan, Rāghib Isfahāni, believes that the word *iqāmah* means "continuation" as well as "performance."[2] Tabarsi, a Qurʾan exegete, claims that

[2] Rāghib Isfahāni, Husayn b. Muhammad (Damascus and Beirut: Dar al-ʿIlm and Dar al-Shamiyyah, 1412/1991), s.v. *qiyām*.

the reason for this is that *iqāmat al-salāt* means performing ritual prayer while observing all its details and regulations.[3]

Another recent interpretation explains that since ritual prayer according to Islamic law is to some extent a collective prayer and thus an important social institution, it also has many social effects. Thus, the performance of ritual prayer in fact "establishes" a social phenomenon.

The beginning chapters of Islamic jurisprudence elaborate the details, conditions, and various obligations of Islamic prayer.

Remembrance of God

Maintain the prayer for My remembrance. (20:14)

According to the Qurʾan, ritual prayer is a form of remembrance of God, the Creator of the universe with all His Names and Attributes known and revealed by Him: Merciful, Beneficent, All-Generous, All-Forgiving, All-Forgiver, All-Clement, All-Appreciative, All-Munificent, All-Affectionate, All-Attentive, and so forth. The repetition of ritual prayer at different hours of the day and night recalls and deepens a devotional understanding of the universe and our position in it. It is important that those who say their prayer engage all their thoughts, feelings, and emotions with this understanding and consider themselves totally responsive to it.

Ritual Prayer a Deterrent from Indecent and Wrong Acts

Maintain the [ritual] prayer. Indeed the prayer prevents indecencies and wrongs. (29:45)

Standing before God and speaking to Him directs us to pay attention to and observe the other duties and responsibilities

[3] Tabarsī, Fadl b. Sahl, *Majmaʿ al-Bayān fī Tafsir al-Qurʾān*, 3rd ed., vol. 1, (Tehran: Nāsir Khosrow, 1372/1993), p. 121.

that we have toward our Creator and His creation. Repeating prayers and attending to what is said deepens one's religious insight and weakens the desire to commit sin. For this reason the Qur'an says, "Maintain the prayer. Indeed the ritual prayer prevents indecencies and wrongs, and the remembrance of Allah is surely greater" (29:45).

Prayer to Efface Sins

> *Maintain the prayer at the two ends of the day, and during the early hours of the night. Indeed good deeds efface misdeeds. That is an admonition for the mindful.* (11:114)

According to tradition, the Prophet said to Imam Ali that ritual prayer is like a stream of water that, flowing over us five times a day, will cleanse us of all worldly impurities and will cause all sins committed in between one's performance of the ritual prayers to be forgiven.

The Prophet said that ritual prayer is like the tent pole of our faith. Just as a tent and its pegs are useless without a pole, so our good acts will not be useful in lifting us up and drawing us closer to the Lord if there is no ritual prayer. Ritual prayer gives divine motivation to our acts and those of the community.

The establishment of ritual prayer indicates the firmness of a religious life in both the individual and social realms. According to a tradition transmitted from the Prophet's household, Islam is founded on five pillars, the first of which is ritual prayer (the other pillars are almsgiving, fasting, hajj [pilgrimage], and *wilāyah* [belief in the divinely appointed leadership of the pure Imams]).[4]

[4] Kulayni, Muhammad b. Yaʾqoub, *Al-Kāfi*, vol. 2, p. 18. The tradition continues that among these five pillars *wilāyah* is the most important one, for a righteous leader in a society guides people to a divine, pure life, while a corrupt leader tries to destroy religious teachings and removes them from the lives of individuals and from society. It is notable that this *hadis* (saying) in non-Shiʿite sources is quoted differently; i.e., it does not contain the last element, namely *wilāyah* (righteous social leadership).

Ritual prayer is a symbol of our surrender to the Benevolent and Merciful God, the Creator of all servants. If we do not do so, it is possible for us to consider ourselves above all others and to regard ourselves as their lord—in other words, to make ourselves a substitute for God and thus become a danger to the whole society.

In Islam the components of ritual prayer consist of pure intention, *takbirat al-Iharām* (see below), standing, recitation of certain chapters of the Qur'an, bowing down, prostration, remembrance phrases, *tashahhud* (bearing witness that God is One and has no partners and that Muhammad is His servant and messenger), and *taslīm* (offering peace to the Prophet, to all righteous people, and to all who are praying).

Intention

One should make an intention to perform the designated ritual prayer for the purpose of drawing closer to God. If one prays in order to show off, or for any other selfish motives, one's ritual prayer becomes void.

In fact, it is intention that constitutes the core of any act of worship; the acts themselves are considered as its shell and appearance. A sincere, pure intention paves the way for a believer to pray sincerely and to gain God's pleasure for his other daily acts and practices.

The presence of a sincere intention when performing even an ordinary daily act changes it into an act of worship and helps one draw closer to God, provided that that act itself is not disapproved of in the eyes of religion.

Takbirat al-Iharām

The actual ritual prayer starts when the praying person utters *Allahu Akbar* (God is the Greatest). With this we enter the formal state of ritual prayer and remain there until the completion of the ritual prayer. In this state we are not allowed to face right or left, to talk to anyone save God, to eat and drink, or to do any other acts that disturb the appearance of our worship. It is as if we are God's special guests and under His special attention and care.

It is recommended that when we pray we raise our palms to the level of our ears while uttering *Takbirat al-Iharām*. This act symbolizes that we throw behind ourselves whatever is not God and concentrate our full attention on our Lord.

Standing (*Qiyām*)

One should perform the primary part of each unit (*rakʾat*) of ritual prayer in a standing position, unless one is unable to stand because of sickness or some other reason. We begin in a standing position, and then as we continue praying, our humility increases and we bow down and prostrate ourselves before God. Uttering *Takbirat al-Iharām* and reciting must be performed in the standing position. Standing symbolizes turning to God and turning away from anything that is not God; it also symbolizes our acceptance of the principles and fundamentals of a religious worldview and our leaving behind the laziness and indolence that stand in the way of gaining religious and spiritual insight.

Recitation

In the first two units of each ritual prayer one should recite the opening chapter of the Qurʾan—this is a very important part of daily prayers—and another chapter, such as chapter 112.[5]

The opening chapter consists of seven verses containing a concise statement of the Islamic worldview and Qurʾanic knowledge. It is appropriate here to have a glance at this chapter:

[5] There are four exceptions: chapters 32, 41, 53, and 96. In each of these chapters there is a verse directing one to prostrate on hearing it. It is not permissible to recite these chapters in one's prayer.

> In the Name of God, the All-beneficent, the All-merciful. All praise belongs to God, Lord of all the worlds, the All-beneficent, the All-merciful, Master of the Day of Retribution. You [alone] do we worship, and to You [alone] do we turn for help. Guide us on the straight path, the path of those whom You have blessed—such as have not incurred Your wrath, nor are astray.

Like other chapters of the Qurʾan, it begins with God's Name and His two main Attributes: Merciful and Compassionate. Exegetes say that the first Attribute suggests that God's Mercy is comprehensive, encompassing all creatures, including even those human beings who disbelieve in God and violate His laws. These exegetes hold that the second Attribute indicates God's special Mercy, which is exclusively for true believers in this world and in the world to come.

The opening chapter can be divided into two main parts. In the first part the praying person concentrates his attention only on God. He glorifies Him as the Lord of the worlds and once more mentions His two main Attributes: Merciful and Compassionate. He then declares that God is the Lord of the Day of Judgment. In so doing, he remembers that the world will come to an end on that day. All will be raised from the dead and presented before God, who will decide their individual fates according to their beliefs and deeds in this world. Almost one fourth of the Qurʾanic verses deal with eschatology and note that on the Day of Judgment God's dominance over the whole world will be made manifest to all.

Then the person who is praying refers to himself and his fellow creatures. He addresses God and says, "*Only Thee* we worship and *only from Thee* do we request help." In the Qurʾanic view, worship is not just praising God, glorifying Him, and bowing down to Him. It also entails denial of any kind of dominance, authority, sovereignty, and legislation that does not come from God.

In the second part of this chapter the praying person asks God to guide him to the Right Path, namely "the path of those whom You have blessed" (1:7). Examples of those who have been guided and blessed are the prophets, their vicegerents, the martyrs, and those who do good.[6]

According to the Qurʾanic worldview, God has established a bond with human beings and has directly guided them. This guidance has been implemented through sending His message to humankind. The prophets who conveyed God's message to people were role models and concrete manifestations of God's message. Basically, the main goal of the Qurʾan in mentioning the life of the prophets is not just to review history or even to give a religious interpretation of the legislation regarding human activities. Instead, the main goal is to explain the way a true believer is to live in human society. For this reason Qurʾanic references to prophets and previous nations are characterized by selectivity and repetition. By recalling the blessed in daily prayer, we constantly have a look at these role models. In the rest of the last verse two other groups of people are depicted:

1. Those who are ungrateful for God's guidance and disobey Him. This group has brought God's wrath upon itself.
2. Those who have lost the Right Path; even though on many occasions they have not intended to disobey God's command, they have still gone astray.

Bowing Down (*Rukūʾ*)

At this stage, and after reciting another short chapter of the Qurʾan, the praying person bows down before God, placing his palms on his knees. Thus far, he has recognized the main components of religious insight, offered devotion, and asked for God's guidance. Now he expresses humility as he glorifies God, saying, "Glory be to my Great Lord, and I am praising Him."

[6] This commentary is based on another verse in the Qurʾan that indicates obvious cases of those humans who enjoy divine guidance: "Whoever obeys Allah and the Apostle—they are with those whom Allah has blessed, including the prophets and the truthful, the martyrs and the righteous, and excellent companions are they!" (4:69).

Prostration

After bowing down and praying that God may hear the praise of one who praises Him, the praying person prostrates himself; that is, he puts his forehead, palms, knees, and big toes on the ground and says, "Glory be to my Most Exalted Lord, and I am praising Him."

This phrase is slightly different from the one used when bowing down, but it too gives glory to God and praises Him. Here the servant's humble submission to God increases and reaches its climax.

The position of prostration is the ultimate expression of a praying person's humility before God. According to the traditions reported by Shiʿite hadith transmitters, when one prostrates, one is closest to God.[7] This is the position that is most appropriate for offering God ritual prayers of supplication for one's needs. According to Islamic teaching, it is not permissible to bow down in prostration before anyone but God.

Humility before God, who infinitely possesses the totality of perfection, is indeed equivalent to gaining access to the origin of endless greatness, and this is the beginning of our spiritual exaltation. After uttering the remembrance phrase in prostration, the praying person sits up and repeats the prostration and then sits up one more time. At this point the first unit (*rakʾat*) of the ritual prayer is finished.

Each ritual prayer consists of two to four units. The morning ritual prayer (*fajr*) consists of two units, the noon (*zuhr*) and afternoon (*ʿasr*) ritual prayers consist of four units each, the sunset ritual prayer (*maghrib*) consists of three units, and the evening ritual prayer (*ʿishaʾ*) consists of four units.

[7] The eighth Imam was quoted as saying, "The closest state of a servant to his Lord is when he is in prostration, because God, glorified is He, says, 'but prostrate and draw near [to God].'" Kulayni, Muhammad b. Yaʾqoub, *Al-Kāfi*, vol. 3 (Tehran: Dar al-Kutub al-Islamiyyah, 1365/1986), p. 264. In this position the one who prays is advised to supplicate God and express his or her needs to Almighty God.

Qunūt

In the second unit (*rakʾat*), after the recitation and before bowing down, those who are praying raise their hands, palms lifted upward, and begin to supplicate God in whatever way they like, asking Him for whatever they want in this world or in the afterlife—or preferably, in both. According to many Shiʿite scholars, we can make our supplications to God even in our own language rather than in Arabic.

Tashahhud

At the end of the second unit and also at the end of the last unit, the ritual prayers continue by bearing witness that God is One and has no partners and that Muhammad is His servant and messenger, with salutations upon him and his household. This act, which is called *tashahhud*, is the only part of the ritual prayer in which both a man's name and his household are mentioned. This shows the significance of the Prophet and his pure household in Islamic teachings. There is no difference between Shiʿa Muslims and Sunni Muslims in this regard. The difference has to do with whom they include among the members of the Prophet's household. All Muslims agree that Fatimah, the daughter of the Prophet, Imam Ali, and their sons, Imam Hasan and Imam Husayn, are members of his household. The Shiʿa believe that there are twelve successors to the Prophet, the pure Imams, the first of whom is Imam Ali and the last of whom is Imam Mahdi. After the Prophet, the Shiʿa rank these Imams, as well as Lady Fatimah, higher than any other human beings. They are infallible, and according to the Hadith of Thaqalayn, as long as Muslims hold on to them and the Book of God, they will not go astray. The Shiʿa believe the twelfth Imam is still alive but protected by God and kept hidden until preparations are made for his reappearance.

After they perform their ritual prayers, the Shiʿa pray for the Imam's health and reappearance.

According to the Shiʿa point of view, the existence of those guides who have a special relationship with God, the One, and are infallible, who are intercessors between humans and the Lord, having selflessly spent their lives in order to convey the divine message to human beings, is one of the indications of a religious worldview. It is a religious obligation to love them and to pattern our lives on theirs. According to the Qurʾan, love for and submission to the Prophet's household is a reward the Prophet receives from believers for his prophethood.[8] Therefore, the other relatives of the Prophet who do not have the levels of faith and knowledge that make it possible for them to be included in the Qurʾan are not considered as members of his household mentioned in *tashahhud*.

As mentioned above, in three-unit and four-unit ritual prayers, *tashahhud* is performed in both the second unit and the last unit after prostrations.

Offering Peace (*Taslīm*)

The ritual prayers are ended by *tashahhud* and by offering peace to the Prophet, to all the righteous servants of God, and to all who are engaged in ritual prayers. After *taslīm* the praying person returns to his ordinary state.

According to Shiʿa jurisprudence, this part of ritual prayer consists of three sentences. In the first sentence one offers peace to the Prophet. This action establishes a relation between the praying person and the Prophet and is as a token of respect for and gratitude toward the Prophet, who tolerated severe hardships in order to shower human beings with spirituality, freedom of spirit, purity, piety, and high moral traits, as well as to free them from idol worshiping, moral impurity, and love of money.

[8] "Say, 'I do not ask you any reward for it except love of [my] relatives' " (42:23); "Say, 'Whatever reward I may have asked you is for your own good' " (34:47); "Say, 'I do not ask you any reward for it, except that anyone who wishes should take the way to his Lord' " (25:57).

In the second sentence one offers peace to oneself and to all righteous people, thus showing that one considers oneself among them and in their direction, which in itself is an inspiring idea. In the third sentence one offers peace to all who are taking part in ritual prayer.

Chapter 4

Public Prayer

A Monastic Perspective on Public Prayer

Notker Wolf, OSB

We were boarding a plane in Bangkok. In front of me two men spread a newspaper, knelt on it, and said their prayers. The people in the queue had to wait. It was time for the Muslims to pray. At first the engineer from Munich was annoyed, but soon his irritation changed to respect.

Three years ago, a Moroccan scientist brought me from the Trappist monastery at Midelt to the airport at Fez. I had some time, so we waited together in the coffee bar. Suddenly, he excused himself and went to the prayer corner. It was time for prayer. Then he returned to my table.

In my home village it is time to pray when at midday and in the evening the *Angelus* bell rings. Going back further, in his Rule Saint Benedict says that when the signal is given, the monk should drop everything and go with measured step to the common prayer (RB 22.6).

What Is Prayer?

Today in the West, when someone speaks about prayer, he or she is usually thinking of private prayer and understands this prayer as asking for something. This is a very ancient understanding of prayer and a sign of our dependence on God, particularly in times of need.

Prayer corresponds to the human basic condition. When we pray, we admit that we have only limited control over our life. We did not determine our own beginning, nor do we necessarily need to continue to exist. The philosopher Heidegger spoke of our sense of homelessness. We live, it is true, in the world, but we created neither ourselves nor this world. For Camus, this was a complete absurdity: we want to decide everything and to do everything by ourselves, but at the same time we realize that our limitations make this impossible.

To pray is to recognize these limitations and to accept them in humility. When we pray, our being acquires meaning and we gain a place, an at-homeness, in the world. The world not only comes from the hand of God; it remains in the hand of God. Thus, those who pray are sheltered in this world. They know that they are intended for God, a God who cares for them. Prayer is an articulation and realization of an already existing relationship with God. It is a concrete acceptance of our relationship with the Creator.

Modern men and women are characterized by a desire to be god, to do everything themselves, no longer serving, but being free to decide everything for themselves. Because they block out the wider, transcendental perspective, they can no longer make any sense of their lives. They can no longer pray, because they no longer want to pray.

Those who pray do more than display humility. From their knowledge and experience of God's enfolding care, they develop a deep trust in God, the one who supports, who carries this world and its life.

Trust gives human warmth to life. In saying "Yes" to this world, those who pray can accept themselves and trust in life.

As the psalmist says, "You hem me in, behind and before, and lay your hand upon me" (Ps 139:5).

Who Prays?

In keeping with contemporary individualism in Western culture, prayer is often seen as a purely private matter, reserved, as it were, for one's private space. This attitude goes so far that not only is prayer regarded as a private affair, but in certain secular circles there exist efforts to ban public prayer and the public display of religious symbols. It is true that Jesus said that when we pray, we should go into our room and shut the door and pray to our Father who is in secret (see Matt 6:6). Here, though, he was not thinking of a privatization of prayer; he was taking a stand against prayer as showing-off. He himself participated in the temple liturgies and lived the Jewish tradition of praying the psalms of the Tanakh, the Jewish Bible.

The first Christians continued this tradition and went to the temple for these prayers at a time when they had not yet separated themselves from the Jews. They took up Saint Paul's call in the first letter to the Thessalonians to "pray without ceasing" (5:17).

The tendency to see human beings only in terms of their individual relationship to God is a result of modern intellectual history, which places such emphasis on human individuality. From the beginning, the church understood itself as the new people of God; whoever is baptized is baptized into this community. This community is the Body of Christ and prays along with its head, Jesus Christ. His Spirit continues to work in the church and prays in her. Christian prayer is primarily church prayer. Saint Benedict permits his monks to pray privately, but after the community prayer. And this private prayer, he says, should not last too long. Public, communal prayer comes first.

Despite Saint Paul's injunction, it is not possible for a person to pray without ceasing. People need time for other things. From this arose very early the practice of dedicating certain crucial moments of the day to prayer. In this way the whole day is grounded in prayer. The psalms already reflect this practice in the Jewish tradition: "Seven times a day I praise you" (Ps 119:164). Thus, Christians of the first centuries structured their prayer to coincide with the main points of the day: morning and evening praise, but prayer also at the third, sixth, and ninth hours, according to the way of calculating time current in that era. They also rose at night for prayer. In Jerusalem the faithful gathered very early in the basilica for morning praise. Those who were unable to attend recited the prayers at home.

The Eucharist remains the central liturgy, a prayer of thanksgiving for salvation and the remembrance of the death and resurrection of Jesus Christ. Jesus' own injunction to "do this in remembrance of me" (1 Cor 11:24) made this a public liturgy right from the beginning. In the same way, the Liturgy of the Hours, as it has come to be called, shared the same public character—which it still has in the liturgy of the Orthodox churches. The former abbot of the monastery Simonos-Petros on Mount Athos told me that the specifically Orthodox element consists in the fact that not only does the community actually present sing the praises of God, but all Christians of all centuries are included, as are, in particular, the saints and the angels. Saint Benedict urges his monks to sing their praise worthily because they are standing before God and the angels (RB 19.5).

In the West, however, the Liturgy of the Hours became the prayer of monks, who began to appear in the third century, and of the clergy. Monks devoted a great deal of time to praying the psalms; in Egypt, for example, they prayed the full 150 psalms of the Psalter daily. Since normal Christians could not do this, they were increasingly represented by the monks. This is one of the origins of the obligation on monks and priests to pray the Liturgy of the Hours.

Given the European climate, monks needed more time for work in order to make a living. Thus, the father of Western monasticism, Saint Benedict, gave the day a definite structure of prayer, reading, and manual work, distributing the Psalter over one week. But in doing this, he retained the old division into prayers during the night or in the early morning (called Vigils or Matins), then Lauds, Prime, Terce, Sext, None, Vespers, and Compline. The reforms following the Second Vatican Council have made it possible, in the light of modern living conditions, to spread the 150 psalms over two or four weeks.

In all cases the Liturgy of the Hours is understood as the prayer of the whole church. In the Rule of Benedict one finds the expression *sicut psallit ecclesia Romana*—as the Roman Church prays (RB 13.10). Prayer in a monastery is not only the prayer of a particular community; it represents the whole church. This became particularly clear to me a week ago when I was praying in choir with monks and nuns in Togo and Burkina Faso and then, three days later, once again here at Sant'Anselmo.

Structure of the Liturgy of the Hours

I have several times mentioned the psalms as the constitutive element of the Liturgy of the Hours. But these prayers also include introductory verses, hymns, scriptural readings, responsories, short verse chants, and canticles from the Old and New Testaments. Morning and Evening Prayer conclude with the Lord's Prayer (the Our Father). These two Offices finish with general intercessions, a final prayer, and a blessing. The smaller hours have shorter endings. The Office of Vigils or Matins is essentially an Office of readings with a reading from the Bible as well as a reading from a spiritual writer, in particular from the fathers of the church. For beginners and for others who are not familiar with this form of prayer, it may all seem rather confusing, but there is a logic to the order in which each hour is arranged that soon becomes understandable. In the final analysis, this collection of texts and prayers goes back to the instruction of the apostle Paul, who wrote, "Be filled with the Spirit, as you sing psalms and hymns and spiritual songs among yourselves, singing and making melody to the Lord in your hearts, giving thanks to God the Father at all times and for everything in the name of our Lord Jesus Christ" (Eph 5:18-20; see Col 3:16-17).

To promote interior participation, most monasteries today sing in the local language, but some still sing in Latin, the ancient language of the Western church.

The Psalms, Kernel of the Liturgy of the Hours

The psalms are the basic material of our praying. These songs of the people of Israel, as contained in the Old Testament, are a treasury of prayers of high literary quality and spiritual sensitivity. Full of trust, the psalmist turns to God in the midst of every kind of distress, in sickness, in persecution, in times of betrayal, always confident that in the end God will stand by him. Again, he bursts into joyful song because of a victory or to celebrate the greatness of God as shown in the wonders of creation. Some psalms tell the story of the deliverance of the people of Israel from Egyptian captivity. This deliverance peaks in the covenant that God makes with the descendants of Abraham. God has chosen this people and will always stand by them, even when they are untrue to him. For Christians, this story is a preparation for and an image of the salvation and deliverance of humanity from the prison of sin through Jesus Christ.

The people of the first covenant expand to include the people of the new covenant. It is always the people of God that is speaking. Thus, the psalms are prayers in which individual believers can find themselves inside their praying church. They discover that their individual, personal reality is addressed, but with it the reality of the church is also addressed.

Without doubt, the psalms and other songs of praise are high points of human prayer. In the sight of God we can look beyond all human need to the glory of God and glimpse our own future after death. We are drawn up into the glory of God. After my election as archabbot of Sankt Ottilien in Bavaria, I had to choose a motto. Spontaneously, I chose *Jubilate Deo*, "Praise God!" I did this in gratitude for my life, for my vocation, for the greatness of creation, for all the goodness that God has shown to all people, for the grace of salvation, and for the gift of our adoption as children of God. Our sins pale in view of the glory of God.

Praying the Psalms

As their name and origin suggest, the psalms are songs. They need to be sung. Moreover, as expressed in a phrase attributed to Saint Augustine, "Those who sing pray twice." The structure of the psalms in two- and three-verse stanzas indicates how they are to be sung. They are not constructed like hymns, but in a typically Semitic way they circle around a thought or idea. When Gregorian chant is used, they are sung to a number of different "psalm tones," or "modes." In the course of the communal singing of the psalms, the practice of antiphonal recitation by two groups developed, with one side of the choir singing a verse of the psalm and the other the next verse, and so on. It is also possible for a smaller group or a soloist to sing a psalm while the whole choir responds with a sung phrase after every two or three verses. The so-called historical psalms (i.e., those that give an account of and/or celebrate certain events) are often sung by a soloist.

Music is there to serve the text, and a sung text is better able to move the heart than one that is merely spoken. Often when the number of monks is smaller, the psalms are sung using not the eight tones but *recto tono*, that is, on one note. This can be seen as the simplest way of singing. But it is always the case that the singing of the psalms is not an intellectual exercise. As in *lectio divina*, this singing is a way of "chewing the cud" of the text in such a way that "our minds are in harmony with our voices," as Saint Benedict says (RB 19.7).

But at the same time, we are not simply talking about individual prayer: it is the community that is singing. The individual's thoughts can be someplace else, but the prayer goes on. In the understanding of Orthodox monasticism, this is "objective liturgy," the adoration of God celebrated by the monastic community. The praise of God has to be proclaimed. During the liturgies, which sometimes can last for hours, the monks can even come and go out of the church. The important thing is that the singing continues. We monks in the West have a more individualistic outlook, but the theology of the Eastern church is also a help to us: I am "carried" in my prayer by the community, and I help to carry the prayer. This relieves us of the burden of having to be present in thought for every single word. Whoever is present when the monks are singing can, as it were, tune in to the praise of God.

Rites and Symbols

In contrast to the Liturgy of the Eucharist, the Liturgy of the Hours is relatively lacking in rites and symbols. For a long time the psalms were sung standing; one sat only for the readings. Since today most monks are older and can no longer stand for very long, parts of the liturgy are sung while seated. But, as became the practice under Benedict of Nursia (present-day Norcia), the monks stand and bow for the Glory Be to the Father at the end of every psalm. This is a sign of reverence and adoration. At the Sunday vigil the gospel is often proclaimed by the superior in a more solemn fashion.

At the start of every Office, the monks call on God's aid and make the sign of the cross, which they also do when a blessing is pronounced.

I have spoken almost exclusively about the psalms and rightly so. This is because they are the kernel of choral prayer and of the prayer of the church. The psalms are poems on which we meditate in song. After the Second Vatican Council, the number of psalms to be prayed was shortened for secular priests, who are also obliged to celebrate this prayer of the church. The reason for this shortening is that most priests pray the Office on their own, and when that is the case, the readings play an even greater role.

Underlying the prayer of the church is the understanding that it is the community that is praying, the community that with Jesus Christ offers due thanks for the salvation that God has granted us. As we mentioned, this understanding is consciously fostered even more in Orthodox monasteries and communities than in the Roman Catholic Church. But even in Protestant and Anglican churches this basic awareness has been preserved.

These too have the Liturgy of the Hours, even if not in quite so developed a form as in the Catholic Church. This may be because of the almost complete lack of the monastic element in these churches.

A week ago I was at the monastery of the Benedictine nuns at Dzogbégan in Togo. In this monastery the full monastic Office is sung, accompanied by the *kora,* a twenty-stringed instrument that is widely used in that part of Africa. This reminded me of the singers of ancient Israel who sang their psalms proclaiming the greatness of God to the sound of a harp (see Ps 81:2). But what fascinated me most was that this was a group of women who live completely for the praise of God. Here the deeper sense of church community and of church prayer becomes visible. Individuals allow themselves to be encompassed and saved by God in the community.

A Shiʿite Perspective on Public Prayer

Mahnaz Heydarpoor

In Islam, prayer (*duʿā*) is considered to be "the core of worship" and "the weapon of a believer." Prayer is recommended under all circumstances and at any time. God has assured us that He will answer whoever calls Him. Among the different types of prayer, ritual prayers (*salāt*) are singled out. Daily ritual prayers (*al-salāt al-yawmiyyah*) are obligatory. These may be performed individually (*furādā*) or in a congregation (*jamāʿah*), but great emphasis has been put on performing them together as a congregation led by a pious and just leader (*imām*). When it comes to Friday prayer (*salāt al-Jumuʿah*), it receives so much emphasis that all the believers of a town are supposed to come together; some jurists even hold that it cannot be said individually.

The Meaning of Prayer in Islam

In Arabic the term *duʿā* literally means "to call," "to invite," or "to ask for a favor or for help."[1] Technically, *duʿā* means "to call on God" or "to ask God for something." Since we are entirely dependent on God, usually when we call Him we also make requests, and this is why most of the time *duʿa* is used to indicate

[1] *Qamus Quʾran*, the word *Duʿā*.

calling upon God to grant us certain requests, such as forgiveness, sustenance, and proximity to Him. A distinct type of *duʿā* is ritual prayer (*salāt*). In general, prayer does not have any limit and does not need any specific setting or prerequisites; we are encouraged to pray to God as much as we can, that is, anytime, anywhere, in any language, and so on. Ritual prayer, however, needs to be performed according to the clearly defined rulings of jurisprudence. There are five obligatory ritual prayers (seventeen *rakʿah*) that are performed every day, in addition to recommended ritual prayers that are performed daily or weekly or monthly or on specific occasions.

Both the Qurʾan and the *Sunnah* put great emphasis on prayer. For example, we read in the Qurʾan,

> Your Lord has said, "Call Me, and I will hear you!" (40:60)
>
> Invoke Him, putting your exclusive faith in Him. (7:29)
>
> And supplicate Him with fear and hope: indeed Allah's mercy is close to the virtuous. (7:56)

In Islamic hadiths, we read that Prophet Muhammad said,

> Praying to God is the core of worship. No one ever asks God for a favour unless his wish is granted. It will either be hastened—and thus granted in this world—or it will be granted in the hereafter or it will cause his sins to be forgiven as much as he has prayed and that is only when he has not asked for a sinful wish.[2]

Public Prayer

Islam puts also great emphasis on public prayer. Imam Sadiq is quoted as saying, "There is no group of forty people who get together and call upon God for a certain request unless God

[2] *Wasail al-Shia*, vol. 7, p. 27, no. 8615.

grants their request before they leave."[3] In another narration after saying almost the same, the Imam says, "If forty people could not get together then four people should ask God for their request ten times and it will be granted."[4]

It has been narrated that once a group of people went to Prophet Muhammad and said that their land has been stricken by famine and that they wanted the Prophet to pray for rain. The Prophet ordered people to prepare the pulpit and to gather everyone. Then he started praying and asked people to say "Amen" afterward.[5] From this story we can learn that when a group of people asks God for a favor, it increases the chances of its acceptance. This is a fact that has been explicitly stated by Imam Ali: "God's hand is with those who form a group."[6]

Advantages of Public Prayer

God is more likely to answer the prayer of a group in which there is a heartbroken person. The larger the group, the greater the possibility that a heartbroken person is present. In reply to the question about where God exists or can be found, Prophet Muhammad said, "Close to the broken hearts."[7]

God sends more mercy when there are more people praying to Him. Each person can attract God's attention by his or her characteristics. Now if more people pray together, then their good deeds will add up and thus make it more likely for their prayers to be accepted. Imam Sadiq said, "Whenever my father [Imam Baqir] faced a problem he would gather women and children around, then he would pray and ask them to say Amen."[8] In another narration we read, "Whenever a servant [of God] performs a congregational prayer and then asks God for a favour, God is

[3] Ibid., vol. 7, p. 487.

[4] Ibid., vol. 2, p. 487, no. 5576.

[5] Ibid., vol. 8, p. 217.

[6] *Bihar al-Anwar*, vol. 33, chap. 23, p. 372.

[7] Ibid., vol. 70, p. 157.

[8] *Al-Kafi*, vol. 2, p. 487.

embarrassed to let him leave that place without his request being granted."[9]

Learning the manners of supplicating. When among others, a person who is not familiar with the manners of praying can learn from those who lead the prayer.

Being reminded of important supplications. Praying together can teach us the things we should ask for but may not think of. Furthermore, public prayer will also provide us with the specific supplications to be made on certain days or occasions.

Vitality. Doing something alone makes many people tired or bored much earlier than when they do it as a group. Prayer is not an exception. When alone, there seem to be more temptations and bad thoughts coming to mind than when we are in the presence of faithful people. In Duᶜā of Nudbah, a supplication during which Shiᶜites ask God to hasten the reappearance of Imam Mahdi, we read, "Is there any helper with whom I can prolong my weeping and crying [for you, O Imam]?"[10] This phrase shows that even for something as personal as weeping and crying we should look for helpers so that together we may remember the Imam and our responsibilities toward him for a longer period. Such crying and weeping is a very uplifting experience and helps to cleanse one's heart and to refine one's thoughts and intentions. This is a sacred sadness that energizes the person and is very different from the sadness caused by having no worldly means of pleasure.

Congregational Ritual Prayer (*Salāt al-Jamāᶜah*)

Although daily ritual prayers (*salāt*) can be said both individually and congregationally, it is very highly recommended to say them in groups in mosques or other appropriate places. Those who live near a mosque or can hear the call for prayer (*adhān*) from a mosque are even more encouraged to attend the

[9] *Wasail al-Shia*, vol. 8, p. 289, no. 10689.

[10] *Mafātih al-jinān*. See also *Bihār al-Anwār*, vol. 99, p. 108.

congregational prayers.[11] On the other hand, abandoning the congregational prayer out of defiance and with no excuse is highly discouraged.[12] Attending congregational prayers is so important that it outweighs praying at the beginning of the specified time for each daily ritual prayer, which is very highly recommended by itself. Therefore, congregational prayer that is performed later (of course, within the time limit of each prayer) is preferred to a private prayer performed at the beginning of the appointed time.[13] Even if a person has prayed individually at the beginning of the appointed time, such a person should join those who may gather for prayer later in the time period and pray again with them.[14]

Saying daily ritual prayers in congregation is so important that it seems that this has been considered as the primary option in the divine legislation for or the design of such prayers. This can be seen in the fact that many pronouns used in passages recited in each daily ritual prayer are in the plural form. For example, in every daily prayer in the first two *rakʿah*, chapter Opening must be recited. The second half of the chapter reads as follows:

> You [alone] do we worship, and to You [alone] do we turn for help. Guide us on the straight path, the path of those whom You have blessed—such as have not incurred Your wrath, nor are astray. (1:5-7)

Plural pronouns are also used at the end of the prayer: "Allah's peace be on us—those offering prayers—and upon all pious servants of Allah. Allah's peace, blessings, and grace be on you believers!"

[11] *Tawzih al-Masail*, Ayatullah Khomeini, no. 1399.

[12] Ibid., no. 1401.

[13] Ibid., no. 1402; *Wasail al-Shia*, vol. 8, p. 308; *Wasail al-Shia*, vol. 8, p. 401, no. 11014.

[14] *Tawzih al-Masail*, Ayatullah Khomeini, no. 1403; *Wasail al-Shia*, vol. 8, p. 401.

The Importance of Congregational Prayer in the Qurʾan and in Hadiths

The Qurʾan emphasizes saying one's ritual prayers in the company of other believers who are praying at the same time. This has been interpreted by Qurʾanic exegetes as an instruction to attend congregational ritual prayers.[15] The Qurʾan says, "And maintain the prayer, and give the *zakāt* [alms], and bow along with those who bow [in prayer]" (2:43). It also says that God told Lady Mary, "O Mary, be obedient to your Lord, and prostrate and bow down with those who bow [in worship]" (3:43).[16]

In the hadiths there are many passages extoling the merits of congregational prayer over private prayer. For example, Prophet Muhammad quotes Gabriel as saying,

> O Muhammad! If two people participate in the congregational prayer they will be given the reward for a hundred and fifty prayers each. If three people participate in the congregational prayer they will be each given the reward for six hundred prayers. If four people participate in the congregational prayer they will be each given the reward for one thousand and two hundred prayers. . . . However, as soon as the number of the participants exceeds ten, then if all the skies become ink and all the trees become pens, and jinns and humans try to write, they cannot write the reward for one unit of this prayer.[17]

Prophet Muhammad also says that God will give plentiful rewards for every step a person makes to attend congregational prayers:

[15] E.g., see *Tafsir Nemuneh*, vol. 1, p. 209.

[16] Of course, this verse may also be interpreted in a different way—i.e., to refer to the importance of praying to God along with others who also do so—that is not necessarily about the formal congregational prayer. See, e.g., *Tafsir Nemuneh*, vol. 2, p. 543.

[17] *Bihar al-Anwar*, vol. 85, p. 14.

> Be aware that whoever goes towards the mosque for performing prayers, for each step he takes seventy thousand rewards will be written for him. And if he dies in this state God will appoint seventy thousand angels to visit him in his grave and to keep his company in his loneliness and to ask God for forgiveness for him till the day he is resurrected.[18]

In hadiths the lines of people in congregational prayer is likened to lines of angels, and it is also stated there that each unit of a congregational prayer is equal to twenty-four units of a prayer whose units are more favored before God than worshiping for forty years.[19]

Outcomes of Congregational Prayer

Exhibiting values of prayer and devotion to God in society. Congregational prayer exhibits values such as faith, monotheism, devotion to God, and worship; serves as a kind of reassurance for believers; and prepares the ground for others to be attracted toward these values. Imam Rida said, "Certainly, the congregational prayer has been set so that sincerity, monotheism, submission, and worshiping God would be exhibited and witnessed."[20]

Strengthening people's relationships. Congregational prayer allows people to come to know one another and hopefully to become closer as a result. It is a common practice that after finishing the congregational prayer, people shake hands in the hope that it will strengthen their ties of brotherhood and remove any kind of hatred from their hearts.

Although a small distance between people standing in the same row and between different rows does not make congregational prayer invalid,[21] it has been said that it is better if there is

[18] *Wasail al-Shia*, vol. 8, p. 287, no. 10681.

[19] Ibid., vol. 8, p. 287, no. 10684.

[20] Ibid., vol. 8, p. 287, no. 10683.

[21] Ibid., vol. 8, p. 410, no. 11038.

no distance at all. Indeed, Prophet Muhammad advised people in the same lines to stand shoulder to shoulder.[22] He used to tell them, "Be organized. Do not be disordered and separate because that would make your hearts distant."[23] It has also been said that if there is enough space for one to stand in a row beside others, one should not go and stand alone behind them, making a new row.[24] Such rulings are lessons of unity, integration, and avoiding division.

Discipline and punctuality. Congregational prayer disciplines people and helps maintain order and punctuality. The connection of lines that are shaped in rows behind the prayer leader is a witness to Muslims' solidarity and a manifestation of their discipline. Hearing the call for prayer, Muslims, wherever they are, go to the mosque. There the people sitting in their ordered lines stand up and cry, "God is great." Together they listen attentively to the Imam's Qurʾanic recitation. Then they bow and prostrate before God, sit, and stand up; after the prayer, they send salutations to one another and shake hands. As a sign of fellowship, the Imam is advised to wait for others to finish their prayers before he stands up.

Knowing of others' needs and being able to help them. Congregational prayer is one of the best ways for people to learn about each other's financial, moral, and social problems or needs and to find ways and means to help one other.[25] For example, throughout the history of Islam, the mosque has been the place where the poor could receive help from the community. The history of this goes back to the time of Prophet Muhammad. Once a poor man entered the mosque and asked people for help. Imam Ali, who at that moment was performing his prayers, gestured for the poor person to approach him. While bowing to

[22] Ibid., vol. 8, p. 423, no. 11073; ibid., vol. 8, p. 423, no. 11076.

[23] *Mustadrak al-Wasail*, vol. 6, p. 507.

[24] *Tawzih al-Masail*, Ayatullah Khomeini, no. 1488; *Wasail al-Shia*, vol. 8, p. 407, no. 11032.

[25] *Wasail al-Shia*, vol. 8, p. 287, no. 10683.

God, the Imam gave his ring to the poor man.[26] It was then that the following verse was revealed: "Your guardian is only Allah, His Apostle, and the faithful who maintain the prayer and give the *zakāt* [alms] while bowing down" (5:55).

Teaching piety and justice. According to Shiʿite jurisprudence, the leader of prayer must be just (*ʿādil*) and pious. Prophet Muhammad said, "The leader of prayer of every group of people is their representative before God, so choose the best one of you as your leader for the prayers."[27] Through following a just and pious leader in the congregational prayer, people are taught and inspired to establish justice and piety in their lives.

Leadership. Having someone lead prayer conveys a message that people should be unified in their words, direction, and goals. It is recommended that the leader of prayer should consider the state of the weakest member of the congregation and adjust his pace accordingly.[28] Imam Sadiq narrates an incident during Prophet Muhammad's congregational prayer:

> Once while the messenger of God was performing the noon prayers, he suddenly rushed through the last two units of prayer. When the prayer was over, some asked him, "Has a new order come about the prayer?" The prophet replied, "How come?" They said, "Why did you perform the last two units faster?" The prophet said, "Did not you hear that a baby was crying?"[29]

Imam Ali also advised prayer leaders to be considerate with regard to the people, as seen in his written recommendation to his commander, Malik ibn Ashtar:

[26] *114 Points about Salāt (Prayer),* chapter "nazm wa namaz."

[27] *Wasail al-Shia,* vol. 8, p. 347, no. 10867. Also, the same meaning has been stated in another narration: *Wasail al-Shia,* vol. 8, p. 315, no. 10770.

[28] *Tawzih al-Masail,* Ayatullah Khomeini, no. 1485. *Wasail al-Shia,* vol. 8, p. 420, no. 11064.

[29] *Wasail al-shia,* vol. 8, p. 419, no. 11062.

> When you stand with people to perform congregational prayer, pray in a way that is not too long that makes people tired and not so short that it would ruin the prayer, for amongst people there are ill ones and also those who have an important affair they have to take care of. After the Prophet asked me to go to Yemen I asked him, "How do I perform the prayers when I am with others?" He said, "Perform a prayer like the weakest one of them prays and be kind to the believers."[30]

Considering the conditions of the people following the leader in the prayer is so important that Prophet Muhammad said that an Imam who does not consider the conditions of his followers is like an oppressive king.[31] The Prophet also said, "Whoever accepts the leadership of a group and only prays for himself has, indeed, betrayed them."[32]

Friday Prayer

After Hajj (pilgrimage to Mecca), Friday prayer is the largest gathering of Muslims and has been named as the Hajj of the poor by Prophet Muhammad.[33] It has been said that, like Hajj, Friday prayer is one of the four events after which all of one's sins are forgiven.[34] Moreover, a chapter of the Qur᾿an has been named *Jumuʿah* (Friday). In this chapter, God asks people to take part in Friday prayer: "O you who have faith! When the call is made for prayer on Friday, hurry toward the remembrance of Allah, and leave all business. That is better for you, should you know" (62:9).

In addition to the remembrance of God, the Friday prayer has many beneficial social effects, one of the most important being

[30] *Nahjul Balaghah*, letter number 53, "An Order to Malik Ashtar."

[31] *Wasail al-Shia*, vol. 8, p. 420, no. 11067.

[32] Ibid., p. 425, no. 11081.

[33] *Bihar al-Anwar*, vol. 86, p. 212.

[34] *Mustadrak al-Wasail*, vol. 2, p. 61.

unity and solidarity. It should be noted that unlike the daily congregational prayers that people can perform in their local mosques, the Friday prayer is performed in the communal mosque of each city.

Praying is desirable in any situation, since we need to be in constant relationship with God, supplicating and remembering Him. This relationship ought to be maintained at all levels of one's life. At those times when one wants to form a special relationship with God, one can do so privately, since there will not always be a gathering for prayer when one feels the need to spend time with God or has an urgent favor to ask Him. However, when there is the possibility of taking part in public prayer, we should do so in order to benefit from its many advantages, such as the fact that public prayers are more likely to be accepted. Public prayer in general and congregational ritual prayer in particular are given pride of place in the Qur'an and in hadiths because of the exceptional contribution they make to the lives of individuals as well as to the community.

Chapter 5

Witness within the Community

A Monastic Perspective on Living in Community

Julian Pieters, OCSO

> *I am the gate. Whoever enters by me will be saved,*
> *and will come in and go out and find pasture.* (John 10:9)

The day I publicly professed my final vows as a monk, I did enter through Jesus Christ, the gate, and dedicated my life to him by embracing gospel living through the challenge of community living. For the announcement of my final profession, I chose the following citation: "Before everything there is God who calls us and has destined us, here and now, to become community." On the cover of the booklet for the liturgy on that day, I placed these words: "The Word takes this community of flesh and blood to speak out, here and now."

With these citations—the first from the writings of Frère Christian de Chergé, the prior of the monastery of Tibhirine in Algeria, the second from the writings of Frère Christophe Lebreton of the same community,[1] both victims of the violence that engulfed Algeria in the 1990s—I wanted to say that it is not the monk who chooses a community; it is God who puts the monk in a given community for reasons of his own. What God's reasons are will become clear to the monk if he or she listens to the divine voice in interactions of all sorts within community life.

To express my reasons for becoming a monk following the Rule of Saint Benedict and living a contemplative life in a monastic community, I chose the following Scripture texts for the liturgy on the day of my vows:

> For my thoughts are not your thoughts,
> nor are your ways my ways, says the LORD.
> For as the heavens are higher than the earth,
> so are my ways higher than your ways
> and my thoughts than your thoughts.
> For as the rain and the snow come down from heaven,
> and do not return there until they have watered the earth,
> making it bring forth and sprout,
> giving seed to the sower and bread to the eater,
> so shall my word be that goes out from my mouth;
> it shall not return to me empty,
> but it shall accomplish that which I purpose,
> and succeed in the thing for which I sent it. (Isa 55:8-11)

> Beloved, let us love one another, because love is from God; everyone who loves is born of God and knows God. Whoever does not love does not know God, for God is love. . . . No one has ever seen God; if we love one another, God lives in us, and his love is perfected in us. By this we know that we abide in him and he in us, because he has given us of his Spirit. (1 John 4:7-8, 12-13)

> The next day John again was standing with two of his disciples, and as he watched Jesus walk by, he exclaimed, "Look, here is the Lamb of God!" The two disciples heard him say this, and

[1] Bruno Chenu, *Een band van vrede* (Ribât es- Salâm), *monniken in Algerije* (Brepols / Abdij: Westmalle, 1997). The book is a translation of *Sept vies pour Dieu et pour l'Algérie* (Paris: Bayard / Centurion, 1996).

> they followed Jesus. When Jesus turned and saw them following, he said to them, "What are you looking for?" They said to him, "Rabbi" (which translated means Teacher), "where are you staying?" He said to them, "Come and see." (John 1:35-39)

Little did I know how great a challenge real gospel living within community would be. This is how Jesus speaks about living the Gospel:

> I give you a new commandment, that you love one another. Just as I have loved you, you also should love one another. By this everyone will know that you are my disciples, if you have love for one another. (John 13:34-35)

> Blessed are the poor in spirit, for theirs is the kingdom of heaven.
> Blessed are those who mourn, for they will be comforted.
> Blessed are the meek, for they will inherit the earth.
> Blessed are those who hunger and thirst for righteousness, for they will be filled.
> Blessed are the merciful, for they will receive mercy.
> Blessed are the pure in heart, for they will see God.
> Blessed are the peacemakers, for they will be called children of God.
> Blessed are those who are persecuted for righteousness' sake, for theirs is the kingdom of heaven. (Matt 5:3-10)

In trying to follow the teachings of the gospel and the Rule of Saint Benedict, I saw two faces of community living emerge. The one face is that of practical as well as spiritual support, offering a life of peace, sharing, support, dedication, simplicity and joy. The other face at times seems the opposite and becomes a burden one would gladly get rid of if possible. It offers misunderstanding, sorrow, struggle, pain and loneliness. My life as a monk in a community is about surrender, rooted in a deep understanding of the will of God.

> Try to find out what is pleasing to the Lord. Take no part in the unfruitful works of darkness, but instead expose them. . . . But everything exposed by the light becomes visible, for everything that becomes visible is light. Therefore it says, "Sleeper,

> awake! Rise from the dead, and Christ will shine on you." (Eph 5:10-11,13-14)

Yes, I keep following Jesus Christ because he keeps inviting me to come and see where he is staying, even in the most unlikely, hidden, forbidden, or incomprehensible persons and situations. Community living can only be dignified by living the Gospel to its extreme consequences. Thanks be to God, the monk is helped in multiple ways to incarnate sacred texts, spiritual guidance, and gospel living and thus to become more and more transparent so that Jesus Christ may reveal himself in him or her and become recognizable to others.

> And this is my prayer, that your love may overflow more and more with knowledge and full insight to help you to determine what is best, so that on the day of Christ you may be pure and blameless, having produced the harvest of righteousness that comes through Jesus Christ for the glory and praise of God. (Phil 1:9-11)

The word "monk" comes from μόνος (*monos*), meaning "single," but it refers to more than just a physical concept. It implies oneness through a focused, undivided, total dedication to God. Therefore it means an "I/Thou" relationship.

> Listen to me, my faithful children, and blossom
>   like a rose growing by a stream of water.
> Send out fragrance like incense,
>   and put forth blossoms like a lily.
> Scatter the fragrance, and sing a hymn of praise;
>   bless the Lord for all his works.
> Ascribe majesty to his name
>   and give thanks to him with praise. (Sir 39:13-15)

> Listen carefully, my son, to the master's instructions, and attend to them with the ear of your heart. . . . Let us open our eyes to the light that comes from God, and our ears to the voice from heaven that every day calls out this charge: *If you hear this voice today, do not harden your hearts.* (RB Prol. 1, 9-10)

The monk expresses this dedication to God in the monastic vows of stability, *conversatio morum* (changing one's way of life—i.e., becoming a monk), and obedience. Community living is the way to grow in the "oneness" through which conversion and transformation can take place. The true sense of my monastic life is persevering in living, praying and working together with my fellow monks in firm belief that "where the Spirit of the Lord is, there is freedom" (2 Cor 3:17). And if, at times, I am not able to feel the Spirit of the Lord, then I can rely on his presence in my community.

Saint Benedict speaks about the monk as a craftsman making use of every tool necessary to be a good monk. In the fourth chapter of his Rule for Monks he lists seventy-three tools to be used in the monastic workshop. Guided by the grace of God, the good monk learns which tool to use for each different occasion.

Stability

"If he promises perseverance in his stability . . ." (RB 58.9). Having lived on my own for most of my life, doing different jobs in different places and countries, I did worry about this. But eventually I realized that stability has nothing to do with monotony, fixity, or being pinned down. Rather, true stability is rooted in the monk's unshaken belief in the unchanging fidelity of God. Then stability is not just a question of willpower but an aid in the transformation process that leads to becoming more deeply rooted in Jesus Christ. Only then can persevering in stability become a challenge to live fully in the here and now. Only then can I also experience and draw on the quality of the perseverance of my community and contribute to it.[2]

[2] I am indebted to Michael Casey, OCSO, whose book *Strangers to the City* (Brewster, MA: Paraclete Press, 2005) inspires me. I have drawn on it frequently to help me express my thoughts more clearly in a language that is not my mother tongue.

> What, dear brothers, is more delightful than this voice of the Lord calling to us? See how the Lord in his love shows us the way of life. Clothed then with faith and the performance of good works, let us set out on this way, with the gospel for our guide, that we may deserve to see him *who has called* us *to his kingdom.* (RB Prol. 19-20)

Conversatio Morum

The monastic lifestyle is the realization of my choice to belong to Christ. This way of life calls for continual conversion to internalize monastic values—for example, asceticism, silence, seclusion, celibacy, dispossession—and act upon them in daily life. "*Renounce yourself in order to follow Christ*. . . . Your way of acting should be different from the world's way; the love of Christ must become before all else" (RB 4.10, 20-21).

Monastic life without renunciation is meaningless. In genuine monastic life there is an emphasis on a simple, austere way of life in which normal human desires are but scantily fulfilled. This is the way the Christian monk points to the existence of a richer and fuller life beyond death in eternity. Austerity contributes to the purity of heart in which the vision of God is possible. By becoming a monk, my first renunciation was departing from family, friends, job, and possessions. The second renunciation, which will probably demand energy for the rest of my life, is freeing myself from the holds of my past life and the vices of body and spirit. The third renunciation allows me to let go of all that is familiar to me and to dwell in a sphere of contemplation with glimpses into the reality of heavenly bliss.

Thomas Merton, a Cistercian monk who died in 1968, is one of my role models in monasticism. He writes, "The first thing you have to do, before you start thinking about such a thing as contemplation, is to try to recover your basic natural unity, to reintegrate your compartmentalized being into a coordinated simple whole, and learn to live as a unified human person. This means you have to bring back together fragments of your distracted existence so that when you say 'I' there is really someone present to support the pronoun you uttered."[3]

Following Christ is impossible without shouldering his cross, and it can be a heavy burden at times in community living where nothing goes unnoticed and nothing can be hidden forever. But the opposite is also true; at times I can experience the community as my cross-bearers, like Simon from Cyrene, who was ordered to carry the cross of Jesus (Luke 23:26), but with this difference: my community acts without being ordered to and lovingly bears my weaknesses.

> Then Peter came and said to him, "Lord, if another member of the church sins against me, how often should I forgive? As many as seven times?" Jesus said to him, "Not seven times, but, I tell you, seventy-seven times." (Matt 18:21-22)

Conversatio morum is good to practice as long as it makes me humble. True humility sets me free from my egocentric ways. Then, even though it will only be in my humanly imperfect way, I can follow Jesus, who says, "For I have come down from heaven, not to do my own will, but the will of him who sent me" (John 6:38). Then body and soul, mind and spirit are one, and the community can sing in unison:

> How very good and pleasant it is
> when kindred live together in unity!
> It is like the precious oil on the head,
> running down upon the beard,
> on the beard of Aaron,
> running down over the collar of his robes.
>
> It is like the dew of Hermon,
> which falls on the mountains of Zion.
> For there the LORD ordained his blessing,
> life for evermore. (Ps 133)

[3] *Thomas Merton: Spiritual Master; The Essential Writings*, edited with introduction by Laurence S. Cunningham (New York: Paulist Press, 1992), p. 295.

Obedience

Monastic obedience means an attitude of openness, receptivity, and willingness to listen combined with the recognition that this responsiveness may involve changing one's life in accordance with what one hears. Monastic obedience presupposes that we have elected to give priority to the divine will over our own. The general attitude goes beyond interaction between subject and superior, beyond mutual obedience: it is an unrestricted search for God's will. Being obedient is one specific way in which the monk imitates the self-emptying of Jesus Christ.[4]

Obedience is a blessing to be shown by all, not only to the abbot but also to one another as brothers, since we know that it is by this way of obedience that we go to God (RB 71.1-2).

> The fourth step of humility is that in this obedience under difficult, unfavorable, or even unjust conditions, his heart quietly embraces suffering and endures it without weakening or seeking escape. (RB 7.35-36)

> They are eager to take the narrow road of which the Lord says: *Narrow is the road that leads to life* (Matt 7:14). They no longer live by their own judgment, giving in to their whims and appetites; rather they walk according to another's decisions and directions, choosing to live in monasteries and to have an abbot over them. (RB 5.11-12)

Monastic obedience is a listening attitude, and in order to reach this state I have to live my monastic life fully alert and vigilant. At times I may experience inattention, or even rebellion or rejection. Then self-maintenance and self-gratification become more important to me, whether consciously or unconsciously chosen.

> Sometimes there is a way that seems to be right,
> but in the end it is the way to death. (Prov 16:25; cf. RB 7.21)

[4] Casey, *Strangers to the City*.

According to Saint Benedict's Rule, obedience in community living is mutual obedience. That implies that I will practice self-denial when necessary. In our secular society this seems like madness. Still, it is the foundation on which a healthy, vigorous, and loving community is built.

In my community there are people of different ages, backgrounds, cultures, and languages who live, pray, and work together within the enclosure of our monastery. We can only stay together because ultimately we each have the same goal and strive toward it by following the Rule of Saint Benedict. We have to recognize that being saved from our dark, evil side is a matter not only of the grace of God but also of the love of other men and women.

We all strive to prefer nothing above our love of Jesus Christ; in doing so we pay heed to the needs of one another, and together we bear each other's burdens.

We all are willing to add our strength and talents to the community, and by doing so we are able to carry each other's weaknesses.

> Therefore prepare your minds for action; discipline yourselves; set all your hope on the grace that Jesus Christ will bring you when he is revealed. Like obedient children, do not be conformed to the desires that you formerly had in ignorance. Instead, as he who called you is holy, be holy yourselves in all your conduct; for it is written, "You shall be holy, for I am holy." (1 Pet 1:13-16)

A mature monastic community is a communion of adult disciples gathered around God's Word, looking forward to the coming of his kingdom. During the whole process of becoming a worthy community member, each person becomes more and more their true self as seen through the eyes of God.

We gladly invite people to stay in our guesthouse for a while. Most of the time the rooms are fully booked by individuals and groups of all ages and of various religious denominations, as well as by people who claim no religious belonging. During their stay guests get a glimpse of how we, a diverse group of sisters, are able to live together, pray together, and work together by dedicating ourselves to putting into practice the Gospel of Jesus Christ, our Lord. In addition to offering guests a place of quiet away from their usual busy and often noisy daily life, we invite them to speak to us about any subject they might suggest. It is our way of being present in the church and in the world.

I have always loved, for their poetic beauty, the words Saint Paul wrote to the Ephesians. Since living in my community, I also admire them for the power they radiate as they invite me to put them into practice. I like to see them as the Rule of Saint Benedict in a mini pocket edition.

> Finally, be strong in the Lord and in the strength of his power. Put on the whole armor of God, so that you may be able to stand against the wiles of the devil. . . . Therefore take up the whole armor of God, so that you may be able to withstand on that evil day, and having done everything, to stand firm. Stand therefore, and fasten the belt of truth around your waist, and put on the breastplate of righteousness. As shoes for your feet put on whatever will make you ready to proclaim the gospel of peace. With all of these, take the shield of faith, with which you will be able to quench all the flaming arrows of the evil one. Take the helmet of salvation, and the sword of the Spirit, which is the word of God. Pray in the Spirit at all times in every prayer and supplication. To that end keep alert and always persevere in supplication for all the saints. (Eph 6:10-11, 13-18)

A Shiʿite Perspective on the Life of the Muslim *Ummah*

Abbas Jaffer

Muslims believe that God, out of His abundant grace, has always guided men and women to the path that will earn them eternal felicity and bliss. When the pharaoh asked Moses to introduce his Lord, he replied: "He said, 'Our Lord is He who gave everything its creation and then guided it.' " (20:50). The reason for this guidance is twofold: it is expected from a benevolent and wise Creator that He should instruct and teach His creation about the purpose and goal of its existence. God says, "I did not create the jinn and the humans except that they may worship Me" (51:56). Worship here has been interpreted as a means through which men and women attain cognizance (*maʾrifat*) of God. And as they become more familiar with their Lord, their adoration increases. God says, "The faithful have a more ardent love for Allah" (2:165).

The other reason for Divine guidance is so that people realize their true potential and so that, as they work toward perfection, they are able to perceive God's enveloping love and mercy. God says, "Had your Lord wished, He would have made mankind one community; but they continue to differ, except those on whom your Lord has mercy—and that is why He created them" (11:118-19).

In this verse God clarifies that He is able to force humankind into submission, but because of the nature in which He created them, they possess free will and thus differ in their outlooks, conduct, and dispositions. But when they follow God's guidance, they worship Him, allowing His mercy to touch them and thereby realize and attain the purpose of their creation.

The issue of Divine mercy is an important one when we try to understand the principle of God's law. If people view the boundaries of the *sharia* as a restrictive prison cell, penning them in and denying them the liberty to express their free will, then they will always be resentful. However, if they view these boundaries as a sanctuary that the merciful Lord has placed as a protection for the integrity of their souls, then resentment changes to gratitude. Lethargy in worship is transformed to eagerness.

And indeed, God is not in need of our worship; we are. For instance, when He directs us to go for the pilgrimage (*hajj*), He says, "And it is the duty of mankind toward Allah to make pilgrimage to the House—for those who can afford the journey to it—and should anyone renege [on his obligation], Allah is indeed without need of the creatures" (3:97). Out of His mercy, He made incumbent that which was vital for the nourishment of our soul and prohibited that which would damage it and stop it from recognizing Him and reflecting His glory. And that is a summary of the principle behind God's commandments.

The Nature of Divine Guidance

God's guidance is found within every created entity in the form of its function, instinctive behavior, and predisposition. For instance, God "revealed in each heaven its ordinance" (41:12), and God "inspired the bee [saying]: 'Make your home in the mountains, and on the trees and the trellises that they erect' " (16:68).

However, sentient or higher beings were created for a loftier purpose, namely, to attain cognizance of their Lord, to adore Him, and to strive to live their lives in a manner in which they could return to Him with honor. Therefore, in addition to the inner guidance that they share with their fellow creatures, they received an external and prescriptive guidance through the agency of prophets and Divinely sent Books. The Qur᾽an mentions that Abraham presented his nation with Divinely inspired scrolls (87:19). Moses brought down the tablets that contained the Torah (7:145), David had the Psalms (4:163), Jesus taught the Bible (5:46), and God's last messenger, Prophet Muhammad, left behind the Qur᾽an (6:19).

In addition to the revealed Word of God, the life of the Prophet—his words, his deeds, and his tacit approval of the actions of others—became the example for Muslims to emulate. The Qur᾽an directs, "In the Apostle of Allah there is certainly for you a good exemplar, for those who look forward to Allah and the Last Day, and remember Allah greatly" (33:21); and "Take whatever the Apostle gives you, and relinquish whatever he forbids you, and be wary of Allah" (59:7); and "Whoever obeys the Apostle certainly obeys Allah; and as for those who turn their backs [on you], We have not sent you to keep watch over them" (4:80).

Thus the Muslim tries to understand what God requires of him through two primary sources: the Qur᾽an, which is the revealed Word of God, and the *Sunna*, the records of the life and words of the Prophet, which represent the accurate interpretation of God's will. The sum total of these two sources of guidance constitutes the *sharia*, the code by which a Muslim lives his life.

The Spirit of the *Sharia*

A careful look at the *sharia* reveals that the underpinning principle behind the various commandments, both prescriptive (*wajib*, *halal*) and proscriptive (*haram*), is an encouragement toward social harmony.

Acts that foster social ties and strengthen the fabric of society are deemed by the *sharia* to be noble and praiseworthy. There is a great reward associated with them. In the same manner, conduct that disunites people and causes rifts in society is deemed sinful and dishonorable. Much humiliation and punishment is promised for these acts on the Day of Judgment.

The social responsibilities of a Muslim start at home; God says, "Save yourselves and your families from [the] Fire" (66:6), and "Your Lord has decreed that you shall not worship anyone except Him, and [He has enjoined] kindness to parents. Should they reach old age at your side—one of them or both—do not say to them, 'Fie!' And do not chide them, but speak to them noble words" (17:23).

And after working to create a strong family unit, we must turn our attention to the community and nation: "But the faithful, men and women, are comrades of one another: they bid what is right and forbid what is wrong and maintain the prayer, give the *zakāt*, and obey Allah and His Apostle. It is they to whom Allah will soon grant His mercy. Indeed Allah is all-mighty, all-wise" (9:71); and "The faithful are indeed brothers. Therefore make peace between your brothers and be wary of Allah, so that you may receive [His] mercy" (49:10). And finally, the duty of a Muslim extends to humankind at large: "Remember that a man is either your brother in faith, or your equal in humanity";[1] and "O you who have faith! Be maintainers, as witnesses for the sake of Allah, of justice, and ill feeling for a people should never lead you to be unfair. Be fair; that is nearer to Godwariness, and be wary of Allah. Allah is indeed well aware of what you do" (5:8).

The Relationship of Men and Women with Their Lord (*Ibadat*)

In practical terms, responding to the Word of God has two facets: our personal relationship with God and our relationship with our fellow creatures.

Personal devotion to and worship of God takes its strength from conviction and correct faith (*iman*). By striving to under-

[1] *Nahj al-Balāghah.*

stand the unique, focal position of God (*tawhid*) in our life and by pondering over His Attributes and Names, and thus submitting ourselves completely to our Lord, we are able to bring about a deeper significance to the ritual aspects of our worship.

The act of worship itself takes many forms: the Muslim prays the daily prescribed prayers (*salat*) five times every day, he fasts (*sawm*) for thirty days from dawn to dusk in the month of Ramadan, he pays the prescribed religious taxes to the poor (*zakāt*), and he goes to the Kaʾba for pilgrimage (*hajj*) at least once in his lifetime if he can afford to do so.

An important practical aspect of the Muslim life is perfect trust and reliance on God (*tawakkul*). Since God is needless and All-Merciful, whatever He destines for us has an intrinsic goodness (*khayr*) in it. Consequently, in all states, we are reminded to be grateful to our Lord and to remember His endless bounties: "And He gave you all that you had asked Him. If you enumerate Allah's blessings, you will not be able to count them. Indeed man is most unfair and ungrateful!" (14:34).

We are taught to constantly supplicate Him, asking Him alone for everything we need and want. Our supplication is counted as worship because it is an acknowledgement of our weakness and utter need of God's grace at all times.

We are taught to repent of our misdeeds and transgressions because God is always ready to accept the sincere repentance of His servants: "O you who have faith! Repent to Allah with sincere repentance! Maybe your Lord will absolve you of your misdeeds and admit you into gardens with streams running in them" (66:8).

The Relationship of Men and Women with Their Fellow Human Beings (*Muʾamalat*)

The basic principle that guides us when it comes to our fellows is to adopt humility and to refuse to let pride and arrogance about our own merits overtake our thoughts and conduct. Everything that we possess is by God's leave and allocation;

consequently, it is not correct to express pride in these matters. In fact, this was the solitary attribute that led to the fall of Satan from God's grace, and it is the only trait that earns hellfire. God says, "On the Day of Resurrection you will see those who attributed lies to Allah with their faces blackened. Is not the [final] abode of the arrogant in hell?" (39:60).

God has created and fashioned each of us individually. Nothing is a source of distinction except faith and piety (*taqwa*): "O mankind! Indeed We created you from a male and a female, and made you nations and tribes that you may identify yourselves with one another. Indeed the noblest of you in the sight of Allah is the most Godwary among you. Indeed Allah is all-knowing, all-aware" (49:13). Therefore, a Muslim lives with others in a spirit of cooperation, compassion, charity, sharing, and humility.

In a comprehensive and instructive treatise, the fourth Imam of the Shiʿa Muslims, Imam Sajjad, outlines human rights. Here are some excerpts from this remarkable work:

> The rights of your wife are that you treat her with honour and gentleness. And that you should know that God has made her a source of tranquillity, a comfort and a life-long companion. . . .
>
> The rights of your mother are that you should know that she carried you where no one carries anyone, and she fed you with the fruit of her heart—that which no one feeds anyone, and she protected you with her hearing and sight, and her hands and legs, and her hair and skin and all her other organs; and she did this with gladness. . . .
>
> And the right of your child is that you should know that he is from you and he will be ascribed to you in this world due to both his good and his evil deeds. And you are responsible for what has been entrusted to you in teaching him good conduct, and guiding him toward his Lord. . . .
>
> And the right of your neighbour is that you should be a guardian for him when he is absent, and you should honour him when he is present, and you should assist and support him in both situations. . . .

> And the right of the associate is that you should not mislead or cheat him, nor lie to him or fool him, and you should not trick him. . . .
>
> And the right of the adversary who has a claim against you is that if his claim is true, you should not nullify his proof or abolish his claim. And you should prosecute yourself on his behalf and be a fair judge against yourself. . . .
>
> And the right of the one who is older than you is that you should respect him. . . . You should refrain from confronting him in disputes and should not surpass him or walk ahead of him. . . .
>
> And the right of the one who wrongs you is to put an end to the matter by word or deed. If he did it intentionally, it is more appropriate for you to pardon him.[2]

Humans have been guided by God so that they may live a fruitful and successful life. In Divine estimation, success equals living in faith, worship, and submission to our dying breath and taking the correct provisions from our worldly existence to the next life, where we will reap the fruits of what we have sown in this world.

Our response to the Divine Word and Will, whether it is formed in our hearts, found on our lips, or displayed by our limbs, must be one of acknowledgement, submission, adoration, and gratitude.

> O you who have faith! Let not any people ridicule another people: it may be that they are better than they are; nor let women [ridicule] women: it may be that they are better than they are. And do not defame one another, nor insult one another by [calling] nicknames. How evil are profane names subsequent to faith! And whoever is not penitent—such are the wrongdoers. (49:11)

[2] Imam Sajjad, *Risalat al-Huquq* (Treatise of rights).

Chapter 6

Witness in the World

A Monastic Perspective on Giving Witness in a Secular World

Finbarr Dowling, OSB

I live in the eastern part of Missouri in the central United States where I minister to a farming community on the north banks of the great Missouri river. Recently, the Catholic Diocese of Saint Louis hired a fund-raising firm from Chicago and assigned sophisticated city folk to visit the parish communities. The young lady assigned to our parish called to say she was only twenty-five miles away and would be with us in about a half an hour. An hour passed. Then another call. Her GPS (Global Positioning System) had indicated the correct distance but omitted to make note of the intervening Missouri river! To find a bridge she had to detour another seventy miles. A local farmer smiled and commented, "It's better to be grounded than global."

Imagination

A great challenge to the Benedictine monasteries in the twenty-first century is to live in a manner grounded in their monastic traditions yet to be able to communicate with the increasingly global and electronic generations new to our planet. The social networks of Facebook, Twitter, and so forth, bring repeated moments of excitement and titillation to our senses. They promise more to come—and all before we have time to think, let alone reflect, about the wholeness or goodness of what we are presently seeing. The anonymity of the screen is contributing to an accepted distance of viewers from any true relationship with their subjects (no real blood in them!) and thus from any responsibility for their well-being. While the monastic Rule of Saint Benedict did not envisage such electronic sound-bite people, the men and women in today's Benedictine communities have a privileged opportunity to witness to peaceful and contemplative living in a way that allows others to seek and discover the Creator in the midst of this new frenetic environment. Such a discovery requires an imagination that has been nurtured and formed to believe in the presence of the intangible and the divine.

The English Benedictine oblate and spiritual writer Esther de Waal has this to say about the recovery of the religious imagination:

> I have come to see that the Celtic way of prayer is prayer with the whole of myself, a totality of praying that embraces the fullness of my personhood, and allows me not only to pray with words but also, more important, with the heart, the feelings, using image and symbol, touching the springs of my imagination.
>
> I like to think of it as a journey into prayer. The Celtic understanding of journeying is in itself so rich and so significant. It is *peregrinatio*, seeking, quest, adventure, wandering, exile—it is ultimately a journey . . . to find the place of my resurrection, the resurrected self, the self that I might hope to be, to become, the true self in Christ. . . .

> The essential starting point is the fact that Celtic Christianity was essentially monastic. . . . The Celtic way of prayer was learned from the monasteries . . . [with] no separation of praying and living . . . so that life is to be punctuated by prayer, become prayer.[1]

The great American monk Thomas Merton put it this way: "Imagination is the creative task of making symbols, joining things together in such a way that they throw new light on each other and on everything around them. . . . Imagination is something which enables us to discover unique present meaning in a given moment of life. Without imagination the contemplative life can be extremely dull and fruitless."[2]

The power of the imagination is acutely experienced in recognizing and embracing symbols. A contemporary Celtic abbot, Mark Hederman of Glenstal Abbey, writes that "symbols are particles of one reality which bespeak their connection to, or with, a greater reality."[3] He invites us to experience the world symbolically. Then the energy of the Creator takes over as the operating fuel in human personality. Symbols show the cause and the continuity of life. As one sees the signs of the greater reality, the symbols then also show the result of such living. As a guiding quote introducing his book, he gives Elizabeth Browning's words from *Aurora Leigh*, book VII:

> Earth's crammed with heaven,
> And every common bush afire with God;
> But only he who sees, takes off his shoes,
> The rest sit round it and pluck blackberries.

[1] Esther de Waal, *The Celtic Way of Prayer* (New York: Doubleday, 1997), pp. ix, xi.

[2] Thomas Merton, *Contemplation in a World of Action* (New York: Doubleday, Image Books, 1973), p. 357.

[3] Mark Hedermann, OSB, *Symbolism: The Glory of the Escutcheoned Doors* (Dublin: Veritas, 2007), p. 7.

The monks of today have a treasure of contemplative experience that they are now challenged to open to secular spirits. They need to find new symbols to serve as icons through which Tweeters and Facebook devotees will get a sense of awe, a glimpse of the Holy, which will draw them to further exploration. It may be hard to match the excitement and the sensory immediacy of a U2 concert, but a captivating sense of wonder can be engendered that will lead to later enlightenment. These experiences are indirect because, as the Celtic poet Patrick Kavanagh wrote in his poem *Advent*, "through a chink too wide there comes no wonder."[4]

The Separated Community

The massive movements of people in recent decades have led to a deep sense of uprootedness for individuals and groups. This leaves many, particularly the younger generations, wondering where they belong. Leaving the world and living in a monastic community can appear to be a desertion of normal society. This is not a new impression. Daniélou reminds us that already in the fourth century the monk seemed to be a kind of madman suffering from misanthropy, oblivious to the fact that real man is made for society and civilization.[5] The monks of today can show in living form how the habits of asceticism, solitude, and contemplation and a simple lifestyle call for wonderful social skills and sacrifices and can lead one to connect the worldly with the divine. Monks discover that it is precisely in the monastic community that they find their true place of belonging, their home here on earth, and the signs and symbols of the kingdom of God in their midst.

Central to the peace and harmony of such a community is the role of the leader, the abbot. Saint Benedict devotes a significant

[4] Ibid.

[5] Jean Daniélou and Henri Marrou, *The Christian Centuries*, vol. 1, *The First Six Hundred Years* (London: Darton, Longmann & Todd, 1964), p. 272.

part of his Rule for Monks to a description of the qualities desirable in the person who is the leader, the pivot of the community.[6] He is regarded as the spiritual "father" who leads by word and example. He enjoys the respect and obedience of the members of the community. Such "fatherhood" is usually experienced in the manner of the relationship that young people have or had with their own fathers. In the twenty-first century, however, because of the wars and genocides in previous decades, many young persons have little or no understanding of such a deep relationship. Many are rootless and restless. Single-parent families add further challenges. The Benedictine life pattern is one of respect and obedience, taught and learned in daily habits of regular prayer times, in ritual, in shared meals and property, in frugality of lifestyle. It is one of the ways in which the communities of today can reach out to the youth of the world and invite them to experience the joy and peace of learning to belong in such a "family" relationship. Saint Benedict's Rule shows how such experience can breed a deep and true understanding of humility (RB 7) and then the respect for elders (RB 72) on which genuine traditions are built.

Forgiveness

Another of the great values and skills that the monks of today offer to our fragmented world is that of asking for and bestowing forgiveness. Saint Benedict's Rule for monks is based on the gradual discovery and admission of one's sinfulness and the needed journey back to the forgiving God. Progress on such a journey is built on our forgiving each other. Monks pray often the words in the great prayer taught by Jesus when they ask the Lord, "Forgive us our trespasses, as we forgive those who trespass against us." Saint Benedict begins his Rule for Monks with this instruction: "Listen carefully, my son, to the master's instruc-

[6] Chapter 2, "Qualities of the Abbot."

tions, and attend to them with the ear of your heart. This is advice from a father who loves you; welcome it, and faithfully put it into practice. The labor of obedience will bring you back to him from whom you had drifted through the sloth of disobedience" (RB Prol. 1-2). He urges old and young to learn and show deep respect for each other, even those very different in personality and disposition. An attitude of humility is the key to life in community, and he lists twelve degrees of growth in humility, the first of which is "that a man keeps the *fear of God* always *before his eyes*" (RB 7). The open confession of one's faults before the assembled community, along with the reception of their forgiveness, is an education in humility and in due respect for all. Such a lived attitude would be a magnificent gift to the fragmented and violent societies of the twenty-first century.

The World Today

The "signs of the times," as the revealing pattern of worldly events is sometimes called, are there for all to read. Can the Christian and monastic way of reading these signs aid people to interpret the message of the divine hand? In the wake of the two world wars and the rapid growth of travel on and beyond the planet earth, Pope Paul VI appealed to all people of good will to work for peace on earth. This means first of all "no more war," as he proclaimed to the assembled United Nations in New York in the fall of 1967. If you want peace, he insisted, work for justice; and if you want justice, work for development. He made it clear that poverty was not just a matter of possessions. "There is also the scandal of glaring inequalities not merely in the enjoyment of possessions but even more in the exercise of power."[7] Benedictine monasteries are, like the papacy, experienced over centuries in human affairs. Thus they can speak with the wise men of the day who are searching for a "new humanism" that

[7] Pope Paul VI, *On the Development of Peoples*, 9.

will enable humans to find themselves anew. The way is by embracing "the higher values of love and friendship, of prayer and contemplation. This is what will permit the fullness of authentic development, a development which is for each and all the transition from less human conditions to those which are more human."[8] Benedictine monks of today have the skills to awaken these qualities in people's lives.

Seeds of Dialogue

Jesus sent his disciples out to sow the Word. How do Benedictines plant the Word of God in today's world, and how fruitful will it become? We can use words like "I forgive you," "I love you," "I'll be there when you need me," and "Welcome." These words we learn from the example of Jesus. He spoke a word of welcome to outsiders, a word of healing to the sick, a word of forgiveness to sinners, a word of acceptance to the least, a word of hope to the despairing, and so forth. Monasteries are privileged in being fertile soil in which the results of the Lord's seed sowing can be experienced patiently and personally. Monasteries also prepare heavenly sowers for persevering work in worldly soil. Monks know that ultimately it is God who gives the growth. The monks of today are awakening to the need of really good preaching, yet there is a lingering reluctance to engage openly with the ardent marketers of contemporary comfort and material security.

More importantly, monks are excellent instruments for renewed dialogue within the Roman Catholic Church. They appreciate the pearl of the great tradition of contemplation that the Roman Church has preserved; yet by their secluded living and prayer they are aware of the smug sense of denominational self-sufficiency within which Roman Catholics have lived. A challenge for the monks of today is to learn well the full history of the last two millennia and then to read the signs of the twenty-

[8] Ibid., 20.

first century. These are calling us to allow the Lord to move us forward beyond isolating prejudices, as well as to embrace discoveries and enquiries in space, in quantum physics, and in neurological understanding. They are calling us to recognize the power of goodness present in the many cultural doors opened through truly international sporting tournaments and World Cups.

The Peace of the Lord

Benedictines bring to such exchanges a deep and comforting assurance that the Lord desires the unity of the human race far more than we do. In the Gospel of Saint John, Jesus says, "Peace I leave with you; my peace I give to you" (John 14:27). Knowledge of their own history reminds them, however, of the great human temptation to find security and belonging in their own efforts and possessions, of the age-old sin of pride, and of the quiet narcissism lurking in this century of projected images of self.

An understanding that the revelation of the gift of the Lord's peace is an ongoing process, a work very much in progress, frees us to look again and learn how religious people reached out to the world in the past. Abbot Mark Hederman gives us one example. He writes,

> In the creation scene in the Sistine Chapel in Rome, which Michelangelo completed in 1513, . . . the life-giving finger of God, the *digitus dei*, stretches out and almost—but not quite—touches the outstretched finger of the reclining Adam. . . . Liturgy fills the gap between these two fingers. It is a cloth of gold, a many-splendored dream coat, woven like a cobweb between the fingertips of the human and the divine.[9]

In prayer that is humble and forgiving, monks can be catalysts for revealing the divine in the human.

[9] Hedermann, *Symbolism*, p. 138.

Seeking God in the Now

The mission of monks continues to be that of seeking God in the world of today. An ability to pay attention to the mystery of the present moment is central. A recent Celtic writer, John O'Donohue, describes prayer as "practicing the art of presence." He invites us to transcend the dualism of the human and the divine when he writes that "religious experience is not an escape from the world; it is an affirmation of it. It is a way of standing before reality—the reality that each of us encounters in our lives, our work, and our relationships each day—and regarding it with a passionate curiosity. It is a contemplative posture before all that exists."[10] Monks of today are called to engage with the people of today and then ground them in such vital moments.

There will be no need to rely on technological gadgets such as GPS to give us the security of knowing where we are, where we belong, or where we are going. It can be said that, in terms of Christian spirituality, the "Sacrament of the Present Moment" is the true GPS, God's Positioning System, for each of us. A great sign of the power and love of the Almighty for the secular world will be, in the words of Pope Benedict XVI, "the search by all Christians for full visible unity through dialogue and confrontation in truth and charity." This search, the Pope noted, "needs a more profound spirituality of greater reciprocal love."[11] Seeing such a Christian search reach out in dialogue and love to Muslims, fellow descendants of Abraham, would be a call to secular spirits to pause, notice, and wonder—and maybe to join us in giving praise and thanks to the Almighty One!

[10] John O'Donohue, *Divine Beauty: The Invisible Embrace* (London: Bantam Press, 2003), p. 27.

[11] Pope Benedict XVI, Greetings to Catholic and Orthodox Scholars, Assisi, September 2007.

A Shiᶜite Perspective on Giving Witness in a Secular World

Mohsen Javadi

In Islamic terminology the word *shahādah* means "presence," but idiomatically it refers to the activity of reporting one's knowledge of the existence or nonexistence of something—in other words, the activity of bearing witness. The word *shāhid* refers to the person who bears witness.[1] The English word "witness" can be used to translate both Arabic words. The prevailing usage of the term "witness" in Islamic literature is as a legal term, but it is interesting to know that its meaning in theology is very near to its meaning in law. "Witness" in legal terminology refers to a person who knows something by recollection or experience and can speak about it accurately. In the same way, "witness" in theology refers to a person who knows a truth and is ready to speak about it.

Despite this common meaning, there are some differences in the conditions for good and authentic witness in legal and theological discussions. In legal cases, Islamic jurisprudence usually does not accept a witness whose testimony is based on rational inferences. It accepts only the witness of those whose knowledge

[1] There is a chapter in most jurisprudence books devoted to the discussion of "witness" and its definition and conditions. E.g., see Hilli, *Al-Muhazab al-Bariᶜ*, vol. 4 (Qum: Daftar Islami, 1407 AH [AD 1986]), p. 506.

has been acquired by sense experience or is rooted in it. Muslim theologians, however, basically accept all forms of witness and do not limit witnessing to experiential knowledge.

In general, witnessing is something that is approved, but in some cases it is obligatory. The noble Qur᾿an asks those who know to give witness.

> And do not conceal testimony; anyone who conceals it, his heart will indeed be sinful. And God knows best what you do. (2:283)

> And who is a greater wrongdoer than him who conceals a testimony that is with him from God? And God is not oblivious of what you do. (2:140)

A witness consists of two speech acts: the first is to report a truth, and the second is to announce one's acceptance of the truth. Witness by definition implies that the person who bears witness already knows the truth.

The person who bears witness to the unity and omnipotence of God already knows that there is only one God who transcends creatures while at the same time being very near to them; then, the witness reports this truth and confesses to it in different ways, including verbal declaration.

The word *Islam* means to assent to the truth and to submit one's heart to it. The idiomatic meaning of *Islam* is closely related to its original linguistic meaning: submission. To be a Muslim means to know two important truths, one about God and the second about the prophecy of Muhammad, and then to confess them and submit the heart to them. Knowledge is a necessary condition of Islamic faith, but it is not sufficient, because knowledge sometimes accompanies a denial of the known truth and a rejection of it. Faith means confessing and submitting the heart to the known truth. From a theological point of view, faith is a matter of the heart, and its correctness does not require any verbal declaration. However, from a jurisprudential point of view, one is legally counted as a Muslim by verbally making a public confession of faith. The declaration, if it is made, is a manifestation of the inner faith of a person, but the person may have faith even without manifesting it.

The profession of faith by the public recitation of the "two witnesses" (*shahadatayn*) is in some ways comparable with the Christian sacrament of baptism. One enters the religion through this public sign, and with it one begins a new life and one's previous sins are forgiven. Just as Christians believe that one can become a Christian without baptism by water under special circumstances that prevent the performance of the outward sacrament, one may likewise enter Islam without any public declaration if circumstances prevent it. An important difference is that while Catholics and most Protestants accept infant baptism, the *shahadatayn* may only be recited by one who has reached the age of reason and who does so voluntarily.[2] The two witnesses (*shahadatayn*) may be translated as "I witness that there is no God other than Allah" and "I witness that Muhammad is the messenger of Allah."

Witnessing to the unity of almighty God is common to the three Abrahamic religions, but witnessing to the prophecy of Muhammad is what distinguishes Islamic faith. By witness to the prophecy of Muhammad, a Muslim accepts all his teachings, which are embodied in the noble Qurʾan. One of these teachings is that Allah has sent many prophets to help people reach their final perfection and happiness. Prophets Adam, Abraham, Moses, Jesus, and finally Muhammad are some of the prominent prophets who have been sent to remind us of the importance of worshiping. This is the cornerstone of all Abrahamic revelations. Allah says,

> Certainly we raised an apostle in every nation [to preach]: "Worship God and keep away from the Rebels." (16:36)
>
> Certainly We sent Noah to his people. He said, "O my people, worship God!" (7:59)

[2] However, the recitation of the *shahadatayn* is not the only way that one can become a Muslim. According to Islamic jurisprudence, one is to be counted as a Muslim even before the age of reason if one is born to Muslim parents, and one remains a Muslim, barring apostasy, even without the recitation of the *shahadatayn*.

> And to [the people of] ʿAd, Hud, their brother. He said, "O my people, worship God! You have no other god besides Him. Will you not then be wary [of Him]?" (7:65)
>
> And to [the people of] Thamud, Salih, their brother. He said, "O my people, worship God!" (7:73)
>
> But the Messiah had said, "O Children of Israel! Worship God, my Lord and your Lord." (5:72)

The unity of Allah is so important that Allah Himself and His angels and those of knowledge witnessed to it: "God bears witness that there is no god except Him—and [so do] the angels and those who possess knowledge—maintainer of justice, there is no god but Him, the Almighty, the All-wise" (3:18).

Although Islam begins with verbal witness to the unity of God and the prophecy of Muhammad, it goes further to witness by good deeds and the virtues of the soul and finally by sacrificing one's entire life for the sake of Allah. In Islamic literature those who bear witness to the unity of God and the prophecy of Muhammad by sacrificing their lives are called *shahīd*, which means a person whose whole life is a witness. To become a *shahīd* is not necessarily to become a martyr but to live one's life in a way that one's words and deeds bear witness to Islam by manifesting such divine attributes as justice and mercy.

Sometimes the enemies of Allah try to hide the truth and prevent people from accepting it and from following its teachings. In such a case, the *shahīd* may become a martyr by sacrificing his or her life in order to try to reveal the truth.

Allah says that the prophets have been sent to be witnesses, that is, to draw the attention of people to Allah and to convey to the people what has been revealed to them. This is the difficult enterprise that apparently cannot be performed only by verbal witnessing: "O Prophet! Indeed We have sent you as a witness, as a bearer of good news and as a warner" (33:45).

So the important question before us is how we can bear witness to the people of a secular world in order to draw their attention to Allah and His messengers.

Some people think that a witness in the modern age must use modern technologies like the media or the Internet in declarations of faith. Although using these technologies may have some benefits, it does not help us get to the bottom of the issue.

If the worship of God is the purpose of all the prophets, then the fundamental question is how to bear witness to Allah and His prophets in the secular world in a way that helps people worship Allah.

To answer this question, we need to know what the secular world is and whether it is an entirely new world. Is there any trace of secularism in ancient history and at the times of the prophets, so that we can follow their example in our work of witnessing in the modern age?

A Secular World

The word "secularism" has different meanings, but the common idea among all of them is the separation of public spheres, such as the state, from religion. Secularism, in at least one of its many senses, is rooted in the denial of Allah and his messengers, particularly in the denial of divine law. But there are some forms of secularism that accept God and even the prophets but hold that the realm of religion must be limited to personal affairs and is not to be introduced into the world of politics. Sometimes secularism is accepted as a way of keeping Allah and His messengers away from the pollution of politics.

Here we cannot discuss different forms of secularism and its history. We will focus only on its prevailing modern manifestations: the complete separation of the public and religious spheres and the relegation of religious matters to private affairs.

This common form of secularism is based on the error of making an *a priori* judgment about the nature of religion that limits it to private morality and rituals. But who or what gives us the authority to determine the realm of religion and to limit it to the private domain? To accept Islam means to follow its doctrines in all aspects of life, social and personal. If there are social teachings in the noble Qur᾽an or other scriptures, then it is not possible for a submitted heart to say that because of the separation of public spheres from religion, I cannot follow this aspect of religion. A further problem with secularism is related to the very possibility of making a separation between public and private spheres. Without proper social relations, it would not be possible to conduct one's personal religious affairs correctly.

While some secularists base their view on an *a priori* limitation of religion to the private realm, others offer a historical argument for secularism. They hold that history has proven that when religion enters the public sphere it only influences public policy in ways that are harmful. However, if we have a theoretical reason for holding that religion is relevant to public policy and must not be excluded from the public sphere, the instances of harm that one may argue have resulted from the mixing of religion and politics will be seen as an aberration for which solutions must be found. Furthermore, historically speaking, it is incorrect to claim that religion has only brought about bad results in politics. Whether the application of religion in political affairs will have a good or bad effect depends on numerous factors, including the political situation, the attitudes of rulers, and other circumstances.

Modern philosophy and science, in contrast with ancient philosophy and science, deny, reduce, and at best neglect divinity. The proofs for God's existence are often rejected, and revelation as a source of knowledge for human beings is denied. Religion in modern times is accepted mainly on the basis of personal experience and not on the basis of objective reasons or revelation. The idea of removing religion from the public sphere (as is common in all forms of secularism) seems coherent with the idea of religion as essentially a matter of personal experience. It is not possible to construct a political doctrine on the basis of mere personal religious experiences. The situation is quite different in the case of the prophets who claimed to have received revelation that covered such diverse areas as personal morality and social and political affairs. Because of the prevalence of secularized and secularizing science and philosophy, an atheistic worldview was able to spread and become dominant.

In addition to this theoretical source of this modern, secular perspective, there are also some practical elements working in its favor.

The idea of autonomy, especially after Kant, became a slogan that was used against any religious commitment. I am sure that Kant himself had no such intention, but many of his followers took this understanding as a way to be free from all constraints and responsibilities, even those discovered by reason or revealed by God.

Most of the economic and political institutions of the modern world regard religious engagement in political affairs as a threat to their existence and power. Behind such institutions are people of wealth and reputation and those who have become intoxicated by power. In order to maintain their control, they spare no effort, using the media, the Internet, and intellectual fads, to make people opt for a secular form of life.

When we compare the causes and reasons for the modern, secular viewpoint with the causes and reasons for the denial of Allah and His message in history, we find some similarities between them.

The first reason the prophets of history were rejected was that some powerful people regarded faith as a threat to their power and wealth. Ordinary people were the slaves of these rich and powerful people and followed them in denying religion.

The second factor was the existence of customs that people had to follow in order to be members of society. Customs like these were a conservative element within the society that worked against the reforms proposed by the prophets.

The third factor against the acceptance of religion was the fear of being limited by the acceptance of religion. Indeed, there were those who regarded obedience to Allah and adherence to religion as an obstacle to the satisfaction of their desires. "Rather man desires to go on living viciously" (75:5).

In the modern world, those who are working against the Truth and against religion have hidden themselves behind economic and even some educational institutions. In the past, everyone knew who the pharaohs were. Today, the numerous individuals behind the current financial crises and corruption are unknown to most people.

The tribal customs and ethos of ancient times have been replaced by modern intellectual fashions. There were those who opposed religion by appealing to the customs of the society, while the followers of contemporary intellectual fashions reject religious commitment by appealing to the demands of current prejudices.

Last but not least, the notion of the autonomy of the individual person, which can be regarded as the most important concept of modernity, is often used against the acceptance of any restriction of our wishes and desires. The fear of restricting desires through the acceptance of religion was, and still is, the main element behind the denial or limiting of religion.

The noble Qurʾan refers to atheism and the many forms of secularism as a form of idolatry that puts one's desires in place of God. "Have you seen him who has taken his desire to be his god and whom God has led astray knowingly, and set a seal upon his hearing and his heart, and put a blindfold on his sight? So who will guide him after God? Will you not then take admonition?" (45:23).

The principal and lasting opponent of a religious life is the worship of one's desires instead of the worship of Allah. Augustine had this point in his mind when he distinguished the city of God from the city of the devil. The first consists of following the rules determined by God through reason or revelation; the second consists of being free of everything except one's own desires and lusts.

It is a very unfortunate person who mistakes servitude to his lusts as freedom and who considers following the guidance of Allah to be a kind of restriction or confinement.

Successful Witness in a Secular World

The prophets, as distinguished witnesses of God, always encountered people who denied religion completely or reduced it to something consistent with their wishes and desires.

When Prophet Muhammad came, there were those who were ready to accept the revelations made to him on the condition of their being restricted to personal and private issues, so that they could continue to practice usury and engage in the oppression that dominated the political realm at that time. In other words, they were ready to accept a kind of secularism, which according to their understanding could be combined with religion. But Prophet Muhammad did not accept this proposal.

The similarities between people in the age of the prophets and today allow us to use the witness of the prophets themselves as examples for successful witnessing in the modern, secular world. As the noble Qur'an says, Prophets Abraham and Muhammad are good exemplars for those who want to bear witness. "There is certainly a good exemplar for you in Abraham and those who were with him" (60:4).

Witness as such is a combat with the devil and his forces in the world. By witnessing, we engage in a battle with our wishes and desires and also with those who try to cover up the signs of Allah. Victory in this battle depends on bearing good and appropriate witness.

In the light of our discussion about the different elements of a secular point of view, we can conclude that effective witnessing must take into account the following considerations.

First, witnessing in the modern world needs to be accompanied by rationality. This does not mean that religion must be accepted on the grounds of reason alone, as the name of Kant's famous book might suggest. Rationality asks us to use all forms of knowledge, including revelation, for reaching happiness and flourishing. It is not acceptable to bear witness contrary to the demands of reason.

Second, religious commitment does not mean fighting against all wishes and desires of humanity. *Satisfying* human desires within the limits of reason and revelation is not against religious commitment; *worshiping* human desires is. So, it is important for a successful bearer of witness to avoid extremism with regard to human desires and wishes. Witnessing in the modern world must go hand in hand with moderation and toleration, not with extremism and rigidity. The modern witness must avoid the extremes of liberal secularism, on the one hand, and rigid fanaticism, on the other.

Third, poverty, injustice, and racial discrimination always were and still are among the most important elements behind the denial of the messages of Allah. This is the reason for the hard work and ongoing struggles of the prophets against poverty, injustice, and all kinds of discrimination throughout history. Witnessing in a secular, modern world must follow the same path and not be limited to verbal declaration and academic theological and philosophical discussions among scholars. Our witness will only be successful if we join the struggle of the oppressed against injustice, poverty, and inequality. The Bible says, "Happy are those who consider the poor; the LORD delivers them in the day of trouble" (Ps 41:1). Imam ʿAli says, "I would not have become engaged in politics and would have abandoned the reins of the caliphate if it had not been for the fact that Allah requires the scholars not to accept the satisfaction of the oppressors with the hunger of the oppressed."[3]

Finally, it must be said that, unfortunately, sometimes there are members of the clergy who, because of their bad behavior, instead of being the best examples of bearing witness, become occasions for doubt of ordinary people. It is not good for witnesses to preach to the people to live simply and pass through this world as a sojourner, with light baggage, while they themselves live as though there were no afterlife.

[3] *Nahj al-Balāghah*, Sermon Three.

Chapter 7

Dialogue

Monastic-Muslim Dialogue: The Challenge and the Promise

Timothy Wright, OSB

These monastic-Shiʿa conferences, of which this is the fourth, began when I was abbot at Ampleforth.[1] One of our parish priests in Lancashire asked me if he could bring his Muslim friend Mohammad Ali Shomali to the abbey. We met, we became friends, and I asked him to speak to the monks about Shiʿa spirituality. He opened the eyes of many in that address. In response he invited me to visit him in Qum, Iran.

There, at the Ayatollah Khomeini Institute for Education and Research, I was warmly welcomed and invited to give talks and engage in dialogue. During that visit we spoke about holding a conference at Ampleforth. That meeting took place in 2003 with

[1] This is a slightly revised version of a public address given on the second day of the conference.

the happy involvement of Heythrop College, London University. They hosted an "open day," which was followed by a three-day conference at Ampleforth.

This year, thanks to the support of Abbot Primate Notker Wolf and Father William Skudlarek, Secretary General of Monastic Interreligious Dialogue, we have been able to relocate this conference to Sant'Anselmo, this center of monastic studies here in Rome. This open evening enables us to meet you, our invited guests, and you to meet the participants and experience something of the friendship we have built.

Muslim spirituality is more closely related to monastic spirituality than to any other Catholic spiritual tradition. Both confess one God, revealed in Word, whose creating and merciful gifts we recognize in prayer regularly throughout the day, as individuals and as a community. In addition we read, ponder, munch and pray the revealed Word, available to us as inspired Scripture.

Tonight I want to present three aspects of this dialogue: first, a dream for the future; second, an experience from which we can find a way to fulfill that dream; and third, a pictorial image of how we might find a way to this fulfillment.

This pictorial image is easily described: imagine that the followers of the Rule of Saint Benedict and the followers of the Holy Prophet are like two sets of climbers who are ascending the same mountain, the Mountain of God, but from different sides!

During my travels in pursuit of the abbot primate's request that I examine how the followers of the Rule of Benedict throughout the world are involved in dialogue with Muslims, I have been able to visit many Benedictine and Cistercian communities of men and women in Muslim lands, as well as monastic communities living adjacent to Muslim communities in other lands. Last Christmas I achieved an objective: to engage in *lectio divina* with monks and Muslim imams. All of us who took part found it an enriching moment.

At the same time, through the good offices of the rector of the Beda College here in Rome, I have been able to undertake doctoral studies through the University of Wales Trinity Saint David, formerly known as Lampeter University. As it stands, the title of my dissertation is "Can an Expanded Concept of Memory Be the Foundation of a New Style of Benedictine Community Dedicated to Dialogue with Islam?"

After five years of visits, study, and research, the title of this talk, "Monastic-Muslim Dialogue: The Challenge and the Promise," is certainly a challenge. What promise it holds is still unclear. Two years ago, a questionnaire sent to all Benedictine communities through the kind offices of the abbot primate produced, for me at least, a very disappointing result. Of the seventy communities that replied, it was clear that dialogue with Islam is a low priority. Few have anyone qualified in Islam, and the dialogue, such as it is, focuses on friendship and cooperation in practical details, but hardly reaches into "spirituality." At one level this is understandable: monasteries exist for their local Christian community, and in many parts of the world communities have become smaller as vocations have shrunk.

Let me come back to that "mountain." The One, Creating, Omnipotent, and Merciful God is confessed by Muslims and monastics. Each climbs this Mountain of God using a different track, facing different challenges, while at the same time keeping in touch with each other as friends, "co-mountaineers," deeply respectful of each other and sharing the same goal: ever-deeper intimacy with the God whose Word calls each to climb the mountain. A different Word, a different view up the mountain and from the mountain, but the same deep conviction that the invitation from that Voice of God is to a state of being far more fulfilling than the one with which each climbs. Therein lie both the promise that inspires and the challenge that requires courageous commitment.

Some of you will have seen *Of Gods and Men*, last year's prize-winning film about the Trappist monks of Tibhirine, Algeria. At one point in that film, the prior, Christian de Chergé, says, "Wildflowers are planted anywhere; only God can make them grow." That statement led me to reflect on the meaning of a Catholic monastery existing in the heart of a Muslim country, in the harsh environment of the semidesert, in the undefined no-man's-land of the Algerian civil war. Why there? The Muslim world has many other places that are more peaceful. The Western world has Muslim communities with whom monks could enter into dialogue.

But, as the film shows, in that harsh environment the monks offered the affirmation of friendship, the medical help so many needed, and the economic encouragement provided by their agro-commercial skills, all underpinned by a union of faith in a God who cares, who is accessible through prayer, and for whom friendship and hospitality are signs of Divine Presence. Monks in that environment are truly like wildflowers, but the friendship and respect that the local Muslim community showed them was a sign that God was making those flowers grow.

Later in the film there is a scene showing Prior Christian and two of the monks meeting with Tibhirine community leaders, asking their opinion as to whether they should stay or leave. The Algerian authorities wanted them to move, lest they too be added to the list of Christians who had been killed. "We are like birds on a branch," one of the monks said, "not knowing if we should stay or fly away." With stunning simplicity the wife of the Tibhirine community leader replied, "No, we are the birds, you are the branch. If you go, we lose our footing."

That one exchange underlined the particular importance of that monastic community to that community of Muslims. The monks lived and shared their simple life, prayed similar repetitive prayers, and offered whatever help they could give. They were not grand beneficiaries importing a new hospital or school. A divine plan brought together these two groups, who were, from the divine perspective, both profoundly committed to God, who is Loving, Merciful, and Forgiving. In their respective silent spaces, God is remembered as each was open to the Divine Presence revealed in the neighbor.

Committed by their vow of stability to Tibhirine, the monks still were not sure if they should stay or leave, at least until the violence abated. As Brother Christophe put it, "I did not come to the monastery to be part of a collective suicide." But then, in the words of a Muslim woman—"If you go, we lose our footing"—the monks heard the Voice of God calling them to be faithful to their commitment. The Divine Spirit within their hearts clarified the issue. There could be no departure.

For the people of Tibhirine, the abduction and subsequent deaths of the monks was a deep shock. Their way of life in that semidesert environment became more fragile, but more than anything else, their strong faith in God was shaken. The Word revealed to the Prophet—words of comfort and love, mercy and compassion—had been disfigured: they could no longer share their distress with "their" monks, whose faith affirmed their own. They had lost their branch and with it the support it gave them on many levels.

Today, the orchards and fields of Tibhirine still produce crops, fruits are processed and sold, but the monks have yet to return.

Let me come back to the "mountain." From its peak each of us, Muslim and monastic, hears the Voice of God, but there is an important difference in the way it is revealed. For the one, the Word becomes "Incarnation," God, Word made flesh; for the other, the Word becomes "Book/Illibration," God, Word made speech, spoken in Arabic and written as the Holy Qurʾan.

The way of life of the followers of the Rule of Benedict rests on four pillars: structured prayer throughout the day, meeting with God through *lectio divina,* work to earn their keep, and a commitment to their local community. These four pillars echo loudly with the essentials of Muslim life and spirituality. Here is found the unique importance of Benedictine dialogue with Islam.

We can push the Word of God to its limit: not by preaching, but by sharing; not by teaching about the Word, but by allowing the Word to form us; not by debating, but by listening to the inspiration that comes from the other. That is the gift emerging from the shared commitment to the Word of God revealed to each. Sharing insights into the revealing Voice of God enables each to contribute and to learn. We meet each other not with loud voices and clever phrases but with hearts that have been enlarged by the love inspired by the Word of God. Let us not forget Jesus' encounter with the Syro-Phoenician woman (Mark 7:24-30). She revealed to him a truth he did not want to acknowledge. She forced him to remove the wall that kept out the Gentiles. When walls are removed, a space is created, and in that space it is possible to share insights derived from pondering, munching, and praying with those sacred texts, allowing each to be enriched by the other.

Christian de Chergé discovered the gift of Islam in a dramatic way. During his military service in Algeria, he was tasked with "community relations." He became friendly with a married man of the local community. They walked and talked together, discussing many issues and building a deep friendship. On one occasion, an armed man sprang from the bushes and pointed his gun at Christian. His friend placed himself between them, and said, "This is a good man; don't harm him." The attacker withdrew. Next morning, Christian's friend was found dead. Christian saw the intervention of his friend as a Christlike act of self-giving love. He never forgot that this husband and father of five children had offered his life for the "other." That confirmed Christian's faith that the revealed Word of Islam is a real Word of Love. From that insight each can be encouraged to share that Word of Love with the other and, through listening to the insights of the other, enable that Love to be magnified.

The need to listen to one another points us to regular dialogue and also to an ongoing relationship in community with the other, not just seeing Muslim visitors at the door as Christ but also listening carefully to their words, recognizing that in them, too, we can hear the Word of God and bring those different revelations—God the Word, made man, and God the Word, made speech—ever closer together.

To fully appreciate this, I recommend the words of Archbishop Michael Fitzgerald, that giant of dialogue with Islam. He writes that in effective dialogue each has to move out from their own faith position, undergoing a kenosis similar to that found in "Christ Jesus, who . . . emptied himself, . . . being born in human likeness" (Phil 2:5-7). By removing the decorations of our faith, we are better able to appreciate the decorations of the faith of the other as articulated in their words, not filtered through our own. This experience was confirmed for me recently at a Building Bridges Seminar on the subject of prayer, organized by Archbishop Rowan Williams, another giant of Christian-Muslim dialogue.

The paradoxical gift of Tibhirine was that the assassins achieved something no one else could. By thinking they were purifying the new Algeria of alien influences, they magnified in the public eye the new dimensions that the small monastic community brought to the lives of that local community simply because they were men of God. The monks of Tibhirine opened a way forward for monastic-Muslim dialogue. They showed how the Rule of Benedict can be adapted for this dialogue of spirituality with Islam. Their example offers monastic men and women, Benedictine and Cistercian, a new extension to their existing vocation of dialogue. I will call it the dialogue of monastic spirituality with Islam. An extension of their vocation, yes, but also an extension that only they are qualified to do. Herein lies the challenge; herein lies the promise.

If monastics fail to respond, then surely the climb will be more difficult. God's Mountain reveals the Voice of God to all climbers. Those who climb that mountain cannot afford to close their ears, for not only will they risk falling off the mountain, but they will endanger the lives of others by failing to offer appropriate encouragement. The promise is attractive, but it also involves risk. Refusal now may seem the easier solution, but the long-term risk it entails will return to haunt our successors.

Let us pray that the monastic world, male and female, Benedictine and Cistercian, is inspired to accept this challenge and to reap the rich rewards it will bring. The best view from the top is reserved for those who are willing to take the risk.

Dialogue: A Bridge between the Oneness of God and the Unity of Humanity

Mohammad Ali Shomali

In the Name of God, the Compassionate, the Merciful.

Peace be with you!

I am deeply grateful to God the Almighty for granting me this opportunity to be here with you, alongside my colleagues from Qum and the United Kingdom.[1] I am sure that the time we have spent together during these days and nights will hold unforgettable memories for us and enable great strides forward to be made toward collaboration between Muslims and Christians. I cannot imagine that these things would have happened without God's Providence and Guidance. When I reflect on a journey that started about fourteen years ago when my wife and I and our two children went to the UK for my PhD studies, and ponder about how this journey started and has taken me to different islands in the great and vast ocean of Christianity, I sincerely believe that it is only God who could have consistently propelled me forward through this experience. Of course, any mistakes made were entirely mine.

This experience forms a very important part of my life, and so I would very much like to briefly share with you a few of

[1] This is a slightly revised version of a public address given on the second day of the conference.

the things that I believe have been very helpful to me on this journey.

First, I do not regard this dialogue as some kind of formality or fashion or something that is done to please other people. When I started on this journey of dialogue it was with firm conviction and full commitment to the notion that this is part of my religious obligations. There are various ways to argue that this is a religious requirement from an Islamic perspective. The most obvious is the Qurʾanic call for dialogue: "Say, 'O People of the Book! Come to a word common between us and you' " (3:64). Thus, the Holy Qurʾan itself calls for dialogue, and therefore this is a command for us.

However, in addition to this, I believe that dialogue is one feature of the Islamic understanding of the Unity of God. The Unity of God must be echoed in the unity of humankind. Any other understanding of the Unity of God is not complete. In the Holy Qurʾan, those who divide people are considered to be allies of Satan, whereas those who bring people together are performing a Godly task. Therefore, if we want to draw closer to God the Almighty both as an individual and as a community, we have to prove, not only in words but also in practice, that we are working for unity. This unity can be found at different levels: unity within the family, unity in the community, unity in society at large, and unity of all believers in God. This unity can even include the whole of humanity. However, naturally the grounds for unity will be different. We have more in common with some people and less with others, but at the very least we have our shared humanity as a common ground for dialogue even with people who have no faith. Furthermore, there are many common moral values that we share with those people who have no faith. Then of course when it comes to a person who is a believer in God, there is great potential for sharing what we have in common with each other.

Unfortunately, sometimes we do not fully appreciate the significance of a person being a believer in God. Since he is not a Muslim or a Christian, we consider that it is not important whether he believes in God. However, just imagine having a conversation with someone who has no faith in God and trying to persuade him or her that God exists. How difficult this is and how happy we feel when, after hours of conversation, that person says that he or she believes in God! But then we have people who wholeheartedly believe in God, in revelation, and in the Scripture and who pray, fast, and give charity, but maybe they are not of the same faith as us. We should certainly not take these things for granted or consider them as unimportant. Thus, according to my understanding, working for dialogue is not merely a moral or legal instruction. It is a theological implication of my understanding of the Unity of God and the way in which God the One wants this world to be as one.

Furthermore, dialogue should not be made dependent on receiving a response from other people or being reciprocated. It should be carried out with the same attitude with which I perform my prayer and fasting. If I pray and fast and yet no one appreciates that I do so, nevertheless I do not give up praying and fasting. Thus, similarly I always regard dialogue in the same way and therefore do not participate in it just because I receive a good response. Therefore, I enter into it unconditionally, and it seems that the magic in doing these things in such a way is that there is always a good response—maybe because people sense this genuineness and somehow realize that one is not doing this for any personal gain.

There is a beautiful story in the Holy Qurʾan about Moses and his brother Aaron. God asked Moses and Aaron to go and speak to Pharaoh, who, it should be noted, was a corrupt person by any standard. He killed many of the children of the Israelites and divided the Israelites against each other. He even claimed to be God. The Holy Qurʾan says that at one stage Pharaoh said, "I am your greatest lord" (79:24). He was not content to merely be a lord alongside God. He said, "I am your greatest lord." Furthermore, later on he said, "I do not indeed know of any other lord than me" (28:38).[2] So in fact he wanted to be consid-

[2] Translation mine.

ered as the sole lord of everyone. However, as far as God Himself is concerned, He tells His prophets that they should go and speak to Pharaoh. They should not stop talking to him because they believe it will prove to be useless as such a man is not going to change. God says, "Speak to him in a soft manner; maybe he will take admonition or fear" (20:44). Thus, if you speak very softly and gently even to someone like Pharaoh, there is a chance that he may remember, his heart may become soft and humble, and he may become a God-fearing person.

In today's world, is there anyone who is worse than Pharaoh? Personally, I cannot think of any person worse than him. Therefore, do you believe that there is anyone in the world with whom you cannot have dialogue? If Moses and Aaron spoke to Pharaoh, why should not believers from different faiths be able to speak to one another? Why should not believers in God be able to speak to people of goodwill, even though they may have no faith?

So then Moses and Aaron became frightened. They knew of the brutality of Pharaoh and feared that even if they spoke gently to him, he might become angry and kill them merely due to the fact that they had requested him to release the Israelites and let them take them away. So they told God the Almighty that they were worried about causing Pharaoh to be angry, in which case he might prevent them from doing anything further. Then God said something very important that I think can be taken as His promise to anyone who works sincerely for dialogue and is not something that He promised only to Moses and Aaron. The Qur᾿an says, "The two of them said, 'Our Lord! We are indeed afraid that he will forestall us or will overstep the bounds.' He said, 'Do not be afraid, for I will be with the two of you, hearing and seeing [whatever happens]' " (20:45-46).

Thus, if with genuine intentions we become involved in dialogue, even singlehandedly, God the Almighty is with us and He is hearing and watching us. Therefore, this is a great reassurance for us that we will not be left alone by God if we are sincerely doing something for His sake, not promoting anyone or anything selfish in His name, but rather simply trying to convey the message of God. This is one very important idea that has helped me.

Another thing that has helped me is the Qurʾanic emphasis on listening. Of course, I myself may not be a good listener, but at least I have the Holy Qurʾan always encouraging me to try to be a good listener. The example mentioned in the Holy Qurʾan is about Prophet Muhammad, may peace be with him. As we know, there are various miracles attributed to Prophet Muhammad, and obviously the most important of his miracles is the Holy Qurʾan. However, I believe that what I am going to explain is a great miracle in its own right.

It is surely something great to be a prophet, to receive Divine communications, and to be visited frequently by the archangel Gabriel. Therefore, it might seem completely natural to us that a man like this would not feel happy to have to listen to the conversations of ordinary people. Why would he want to listen to such people when he was accustomed to receiving revelation from God? Most of the people at that time were uneducated, as the number of people who were able to read and write before Islam was less than the number of fingers of one person; moreover, many times these people did not have anything significant to say. However, the Prophet had the habit of always listening to people. He never rushed them, never mentioned that he had an appointment or a meeting in the mosque, or people wanting to visit him, or that he needed to pray. He was always listening, never hurrying or interrupting people, so much so that people were always looking for an opportunity to criticize him. As we read in the Holy Qurʾan, "Among them are those who torment the Prophet, and say, 'He is an ear.' Say, 'An ear that is good for you. He has faith in Allah and trusts the faithful, and is a mercy for those of you who have faith.' " (9:61). They commented sarcastically that he had nothing other to do than simply to listen, and they questioned why he was listening to them so much. Instead of appreciating him as a great man who was respecting and listening to them no matter what, they criticized him! And yet he did not even defend himself under these circumstances. It was God the Almighty who defended him and said, "If he is an ear, he is a good ear for you." It is very important to realize that the Prophet was genuinely listening to people even though this was not appreciated and that this is very far from what some politicians or religious leaders do today when they pretend to be good listeners when appearing in public only in order to gain popularity.

So I believe that if we master these two things—first, to be able to be a good listener and, second, to be able to speak nicely, gently, softly, and wisely—then it would not be difficult to find good partners for dialogue.

I am very happy that I have found among my Christian friends many people who have this genuine interest in dialogue and that we have tried to learn from each other. So I would like to mention my Focolare friends, who were so helpful regarding the first contacts that we made in the UK, and then our Benedictine friends and then our Anglican friends and then our Jesuit friends and then our Mennonite friends—and so it has spread.

One of the things that God helped us with was to document the dialogues that we have had so that other people can also benefit from them. For example, regarding Catholic-Shiʿa dialogue, after we had the first conference in the UK in 2003, with the help of one of the monks from Ampleforth and one of the lecturers from Heythrop College, we compiled the papers in a book. We also asked for some further papers to be provided so that that volume could be completed. Thus the first volume of Catholic-Shiʿa dialogue was published in 2004, one year after the conference. We then had the second dialogue in 2005 with the book published in 2006 and the third dialogue in 2007 with the book published in 2008. So now we have the fourth dialogue taking place in Rome. Thanks to God, the books were well received, so much so that some of them went out of print and therefore we now have new paperback editions published as a set by Melisende, a Catholic publisher in the UK. The first volume focuses on spirituality and theology because in order to start, we felt that we needed to know more about each other's traditions, especially when it came to spirituality. We also focused on family and education as two ways of meeting the needs of the contemporary age. The second dialogue was on reason and faith, and the third was on ethics, for which we had an introduction to ethics in general and also spoke about business ethics, environmental ethics, and bioethics from the Catholic and Shiʿa perspectives. Furthermore, in between our main dialogues we have also had dialogues and meetings in Qum so that the venue alternates yearly between Europe and Qum.

Thanks be to God that I find that there are many sincere, humble, and truth-seeking Christians in the world, and as a Muslim I am very happy to be able to give this testimony to everybody in the world. I take such people to be true representatives of Christianity. Furthermore, I hope you also find in your Muslim brothers and sisters people who are humble, truth-seeking, and genuinely interested in dialogue. I believe that the peaceful and prosperous future of humanity in this world will be built on the collaboration of Christians and Muslims. We cannot afford to ignore, let alone work against, one another.

May God the Almighty enable us to praise Him together, to pray to Him together, and to serve together His children who are the whole of humanity!

Thank you very much.

Selected Bibliographies

Chapter 1: Revelation

A Shiʿite Perspective on Divine Revelation

Mohammad Ali Shomali

Ayyashi, Muhammad b. Masʾud. *Al-Tafsir al-Ayyashi.* Tehran: Al-Maktabah al-ʾIlmiyyah al-Islamiyya.

Denffer, Ahamd von. *Ulum al-Qurʾan: An Introduction to the Sciences of the Qurʾan.* Leicester: Islamic Foundation, 1996.

Firuz Abaadi, Majd al-Din. *Al-Qaamus al-Muhit.* Vol. 4. Egypt: Muʾassesah fi Al-Tibaaʾah, no date.

Ibn Arabi, Muhy al-Din. *Tafsir al-Qurʾan al-Karim.* Vol. 1. Beirut: Dar Ihyaʾ al-Turath al-Arabi, 1422 AH.

Jawhari, Ismaʾil. *Al-Sihaah.* 2nd ed. Vol. 6. Beirut: Daar Al-ʿIlm Lil-Malaaʾin, 1399 AH.

Kulayni, Muhammad. *Usul al-Kafi.* Tehran: Dar al-Kutub al-Islamiyyah, 1397 AH.

Maʾrifat, Muhammad Hadi. *Al-Tamhid fi ʿUlum al-Qurʾan.* Qum: Tamhid Institute, 2007.

———. *ʿUlum-e Qurʾani.* Tehran: SAMT Publishers, 2000.

Majlsi, Mohamma Baqir. *Bihar al-Anwar.* Beirut: al-Wafa, 1983.

Makarim Shirazi, Naser. *Tafsir-e Nemuneh.* Vol. 20. Tehran: Dar al-Kutub al-Islamiyyah, 1374 SAH.

Mutahhari, Murtada. *Islam wa Muqtadiyaat-e Zamaan*. Vol. 1. Tehran: Sadra, 1369 SAH.

———. *Usul-e Falsafeh was Ravesh-e Realism*. Vol. 2. Tehran: Sadra, 1368 SAH.

———. *Wahy wa Nubuwwat*. Tehran: Sadra, 1369 SAH.

Raghib Isfahani, Husayn b. *Mohammad, Mufradaat Alfaaz Al-Qur'an*. Beirut: Al-Dar Al-Shamiyyah, 1419 AH.

Razzaqi, Abu al-Qaasim. *An Introduction to al-Mizan*. Full text is available online at http://www.quran.org.uk.

Rumi, Jalal al-Din. *Mathnawi Ma'nawi*. Edited and translated by Reynold Alleyne Nicholson. Tehran: Nashr-e Buteh, 2002.

Shomali, Mohammad Ali. *Shi'i Islam: Origins, Faith and Practices*. London: Islamic College for Advanced Studies, 2003.

Suyuti, Jalal al-Din. *Al-Itqan fi 'Ulum al-Qur'an*. Beirut: Dar ibn Kathir, 1414 AH.

Tabataba'i, Sayyid Mohammad Husayn. *Al-Mizan fi Tafir al-Qur'an*. Qum: Isma'iliyan, 1392 AH.

———. *The Qur'an in Islam: Its Impact and Influence on the Life of Muslims*. London: Zahra Publications. The full text is available online at www.al-islam.org/quraninislam/index.htm.

Chapter 3: Prayer

A Shi'ite Perspective on Prayer

Fatemeh Nazari

'Abd al-Wahid Amidi. *Ghurar al-Hikam wa Durar al-Kalim*. Translated by Mohammad Ali al-Ansari. Qum: Mu'assise-ye Dār al-Kutub-e.

'Allamah Tabataba'i. *Tarjume-ye Tafsir-e al-Mizan*. Translated by Mohammad Baqir Musavi Hamedani. Bonyad-e Elmi va Fekri-e 'Allamah Tabataba'i in conjunction with Markaz-e Nashr-e Farhangi-ye Raja'.

Al-kulaini al-Razi. *Usūl al-Kāfi.* Translated by Sheikh Muhammad Baqir Komreʾi. First edition. Theran: Al-Maktabat al-Islamiyyah, 1381 (Lunar Hijri).

Fakhr al-Din al-Tuaayrihi. *Majmaᶜ al-Bahrayin.* Tahghigh-e Seyyed Ahmad Hosseini. Al-Maktabat al-Murtaḍaviyyahzaviah.

Feiz Kashani. *Al-Sāfi fi Tafsir al-Qurʾan.* First publication. Dār al-Murtaḍa, 1399 (Lunar Hijri).

Hasan Hasanzade Amuli. *Risāleye Nūr-e ᶜalā Nūr dar Dhikr va Dhākir va Madhkūr.* Entesharat-e Tashyiʾ-e Bahar, 1374.

Hurr ᶜAmuli. *Wasāaʾil al-Shiᶜah ila Tahsil Masāaʾil al-Shariᶜah.* Fifth edition. Tehran: Maktabat al-Islami.

Khaje ᶜAbdullah Ansāri. *Kashf al-Asrāar Wa ᶜUddath al-Abrāar.* Amir Kabir Publications. Moʾasese-ye Entesharat-e Amir Kabir.

Mirza Javad Abaad Tabrizi. *Risāle-ye Liqā Allah.* Translated by Seyyed Ahmad Fahari. Entesharat-e Nehzat-e Zanan-e Mosalman.

Mirza Javad Agha Tabrizi. *Al-Murāaqibāat fi Aᶜmāl al-Sanah.*

Mohammad Ali Sadat. *Akhlaq-e Eslami.* Tehran: Sazman Motaleʾe va Tadvin-e Kotob-e Ensani dar Daneshgah ha, 1372 (Solar Hijri).

Mohammad Baqir Majlesi. *Bihār al-Anwār.* Beirut, Lebanon: Dar Ihyaʾ al-Tarath al-Arabi, 1403 (Lunar Hijri).

Molla Fathollah Kashani. *Tafsir-e Khulase-ye Minhāj al-Sādiqin*, vol. 1. Ketab Forushi-e Eslami, 1374.

Chapter 4: Public Prayer

A Shiᶜite Perspective on Public Prayer

Mahnaz Heydarpoor

ᶜAmili, Muhammad ibn Hurr. *Wasāil al-Shia.* Qum: Ālul-Bayt Institute, 1409 AH.

Khomeini, Ruhullah. *Tawzih al-Masāʾil.*

Kulayni, Muhammad. *Usul al-Kāfi.* Tehran: Dār al-Kutub al-Islāmiyyah, 1365 AH.

Majlesi Muhammad Baqir. *Bihār al-Anwār.* Beirut: al-Wafā, 1404 AH.

Makarim Shirazi, Nasir. *Tafsir Nemuneh.* Tehran: Dar al-Kutub al-Islamiyyah, 1374 AH.

Nouri, Husayn. *Mustadrak al-Wasā'il.* Qum: Ālul-Bayt Institute, 1408 AH.

Qirā'ati, Mohsen. *114 Points about Salāat.*

Qurayshi, Sayyid Ali Akbar. *Qāmus Qu'ran.*

Radiyy, Sayyid. *Nahjul Balāghah.* Qum: Dār al-Hijrah.

Shomali, Mohammad Ali. "A Probe into Wilāyah and Its Social Dimensions." *Message of Thaqalayn*, vol. 10, no. 3 (Autumn 2009).

Contributors

Mohammad Taghi Ansaripour is a faculty member of the Department of Abrahamic Religions at the University of Religions and Denominations in Qum. His research focuses on comparative study of the Qur᾽an and the Bible. He has been a student of Qum Seminary and received his PhD in *Kalam* (Islamic theology) from the University of Qum.

Lucy Brydon joined the Olivetan Benedictine Sisters of Turvey Abbey in England after many years (the last nine in Kenya) as a Sister of Mercy. Besides representing Turvey in interreligious matters—she is secretary of the Monastic Interreligious Dialogue Commission for Great Britain and Ireland—she is Guest Sister, engaged in retreat and hospitality work. Her retreat and spiritual direction work is interreligious in its outreach.

Guido Dotti is a member of the monastic community of Bose in Italy. He was subprior for twenty-five years and now works as an editor at Edizioni Qiqajon. He was cochair of the Forum on Spirituality at the Third European Ecumenical Assembly in Sibiu in 2007 and participated in the 2008 Lambeth Conference as a personal guest of the archbishop of Canterbury. He now chairs the Commission of the Diocese of Biella for Ecumenism and Interreligious Dialogue.

Finbarr Dowling was born and raised in Ireland. Educated in Holy Ghost and Jesuit schools and with an engineering degree from the National University of Ireland, he moved to Manchester, England. After eight years as a member of Ampleforth Abbey in England, he was sent as teacher and administrator to the Benedictine Priory School in Saint Louis, Missouri. He has been serving as a pastor in the Archdiocese of Saint Louis for the past six years.

Mahnaz Heydarpoor is a graduate of the Islamic Seminaries of Qum and also has an MA in religious studies from the Manchester Metropolitan University. She is currently working on her PhD thesis on God's mercy in Jamiʾat al-Zahra, Qum, where she also teaches world religions and acts as postgraduate officer for international students. Her publications include *Love in Christianity and Islam* (London: New City, 2002 and 2005).

Abbas Jaffer is a practicing optometrist based in Harrow and a visiting lecturer at the Islamic College in London where he lectures in Qurʾanic Sciences and Eschatology at the BA level. He has studied at the Islamic Seminaries of Qum and is presently completing his master's dissertation at the Islamic College. He has translated several works from Persian and is author of the book *Qurʾanic Sciences* (London: ICAS Press, 2009). He is presently editing the exegesis called *Rahama* of Ayatullah Hashemi Rafsanjani.

Moshen Javadi is a full professor of philosophy at the University of Qum. He serves as editor-in-chief of the journal *Ethical Research* (published in Farsi by the University of Qum) and the journal *Religious Inquiries* (published in English by the University of Religions and Denominations in Qum). His research focuses on ethics and philosophical theology. Dr. Javadi received his PhD in philosophy from Tarbiat Modarres University in Tehran.

Fatemeh Nazari is a graduate of the Islamic Seminaries of Qum and also has an MA in Islamic studies from the Islamic Azaad University. She is currently working on her PhD thesis on the concept of light in the Qurʾan in the Jamiʾat al-Zahra, Qum. She has taught different aspects of Islamic studies in Kerman and Qum.

Julian Pieters of Koningsoord Abbey in Holland was a teacher, counselor, and social worker before opening her center for breathing, meditation, and aikido training. The teachings of Asian trainers and fellow trainees and a context of spiritual freedom allowed her to give new emphasis to her Catholic roots and eventually led her to embrace the contemplative life as a Trappistine nun. She is a member of the Dutch-speaking commission of Monastic Interreligious Dialogue.

Farrokh Sekaleshfar obtained his medical degree at Imperial College in London. He has been a seminary student in Qum since 2002.

Mohammad Ali Shomali is a graduate of the Islamic Seminaries of Qum and also has both a BA and an MA in Western philosophy from the University of Tehran. He has earned his PhD from the University of Manchester. His publications include *Self-Knowledge* (1996 and 2006, also translated into Malay, Spanish, and Kiswahili), *Ethical Relativism: An Analysis of the Foundations of Morality* (2001, also translated into Malay), *Discovering Shiʿa Islam* (7th ed. 2010, also translated into twelve languages), *Shiʿa Islam: Origins, Faith and Practices* (2003 and 2010, also translated into Spanish and Swedish), and *Principles of Jurisprudence: An Introduction to Methodology of Fiqh* (2006). He is a coeditor of *Catholics and Shiʿa in Dialogue: Studies in Theology and Spirituality* (2004 and 2011), *Catholic-Shiʿa Engagement: Reason and Faith in Theory and Practice* (2006 and 2011), and *A Catholic-Shiʿa Dialogue: Ethics in Today's Society* (2008 and 2011).

William Skudlarek is secretary general of *Dialogue Interreligieux Monastique•Monastic Interreligious Dialogue*. He is a monk of Saint John's Abbey in Minnesota, earned a PhD in homiletics and liturgy from Princeton Theological Seminary, and taught on the faculty of Saint John's University. He also did pastoral ministry in Brazil for five years and for seven years was a member of his abbey's monastic foundation in Japan.

Benoît Standaert is a monk of Sint-Andries Abbey near Bruges, Belgium. He is a biblical scholar and author who taught at his abbey in the international Institute Gaudium et Spes and also at Leuven, Milan, and Bangalore. His major work, *L'espace Jésus* (2000), was partially translated into English as *Sharing Sacred Space: Interreligious Dialogue as Spiritual Encounter* (Collegeville, MN: Liturgical Press, 2009) and brings together exegetical skill, interreligious concern, and a special sensitivity for spirituality.

Notker Wolf is the abbot primate of the Benedictine Confederation—having been elected to that position in 2000—and former abbot of the Archabbey of Saint Ottilien in Bavaria. He studied philosophy at the Benedictine University of Sant'Anselmo in Rome and theology and natural sciences at the University of Munich. He also taught on the faculty of Sant'Anselmo prior to being elected abbot. He is the author of several best-selling books and plays classical flute and electric guitar.

Timothy Wright is a monk and former abbot of Ampleforth Abbey in England. He served in the abbey's school for twenty-five years as teacher, head of religious studies, boarding housemaster, deputy head, and fund-raiser. As abbot, he initiated a series of Catholics and Shiʿa Muslims in Dialogue meetings and publications. He is now spiritual director at the Pontifical Beda College in Rome and the abbot primate's delegate for Benedictine-Muslim relations. He has recently completed a doctoral program at University of Wales Trinity Saint David, formerly known as Lampeter University, focused on possible ways forward for Benedictine-Muslim dialogue.